teach yourself®

instant italian

elisabeth smith

For over 60 years, more than 40 million people have learnt over 750 subjects the **teach yourself** way, with impressive results.

be where you want to be
with **teach yourself**

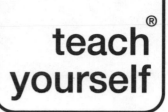

For UK order enquiries: please contact Bookpoint Ltd, 130 Milton Park, Abingdon, Oxon OX14 4SB. Telephone: +44 (0) 1235 827720. Fax: +44 (0) 1235 400454. Lines are open 09.00–18.00, Monday to Saturday, with a 24-hour message answering service. Details about our titles and how to order are available at www.teachyourself.co.uk

For USA order enquiries: please contact McGraw-Hill Customer Services, PO Box 545, Blacklick, OH 43004-0545, USA. Telephone: 1-800-722-4726. Fax: 1-614-755-5645.

For Canada order enquiries: please contact McGraw-Hill Ryerson Ltd, 300 Water St, Whitby, Ontario L1N 9B6, Canada. Telephone: 905 430 5000. Fax: 905 430 5020.

Long renowned as the authoritative source for self-guided learning – with more than 30 million copies sold worldwide – the *Teach Yourself* series includes over 300 titles in the fields of languages, crafts, hobbies, business, computing and education.

British Library Cataloguing in Publication Data: a catalogue entry for this title is available from The British Library.

Library of Congress Catalog Card Number: on file.

First published in UK 1998 by Hodder Headline Ltd, 338 Euston Road, London NW1 3BH.

First published in US 1998 by Contemporary Books, a division of the McGraw Hill Companies, 1 Prudential Plaza, 130 East Randolph Street, Chicago, Illinois 60601 USA

This edition published 2003.

Typeset by Transet Limited, Coventry, England.
Printed in Great Britain for Hodder & Stoughton Educational, a division of Hodder Headline Ltd, 338 Euston Road, London NW1 3BH, by Cox & Wyman Ltd, Reading, Berkshire.

Hodder Headline's policy is to use papers that are natural, renewable and recyclable products and made from wood grown in sustainable forests. The logging and manufacturing processes are expected to conform to the environmental regulations of the country of origin.

Impression number	10 9 8 7 6 5 4
Year	2009 2008 2007 2006 2005 2004

contents

read this first

If, like me, you usually skip introductions, don't! Read on! You need to know how **Instant Italian** works and why.

When I decided to write the **Instant** series I first called it *Barebones*, because that's what you want: *no frills, no fuss, just the bare bones and go!* So in **Instant Italian** you'll find:

- Only 379 words to say, well ... nearly everything.
- No ghastly grammar – just a few useful tips.
- No time wasters such as 'the pen of my aunt...'.
- No phrase book phrases for when you have a tooth extracted in Tuscany.
- No need to be perfect. Mistakes won't spoil your success.

I've put some 30 years of teaching experience into this course. I know how people learn. I also know how long they are motivated by a new project (a few weeks) and how little time they can spare to study each day (½ hour). That's why you'll complete **Instant Italian** in six weeks and get away with 35 minutes a day.

Of course there is some learning to do, but I have tried to make it as much fun as possible, even when it is boring. You'll meet Tom and Kate Walker on holiday in France. They do the kind of things you need to know about: shopping, eating out and getting about. Tom and Kate speak **Instant Italian** all the time, even to each other. What paragons of virtue!

To get the most out of this course, there are only two things you really should do:

- Follow the **Day-by-day guide** as suggested. Please don't skip bits and short-change your success. Everything is there for a reason.
- If you are a complete beginner, buy the recording that accompanies this book. It will get you to speak faster and with confidence.

When you have filled in your **Certificate** at the end of the book and can speak **Instant Italian**, I would like to hear from you. You can write to me care of Hodder & Stoughton Educational.

how this book works

Instant Italian has been structured for your rapid success. This is how it works:

Day-by-day guide Stick to it. If you miss a day, add one.

Dialogues Follow Tom and Kate through Italy. The English of Weeks 1–3 is in 'Italian-speak' to get you tuned in.

New words Don't fight them, don't skip them – learn them! The Flash cards will help you.

Good news grammar After you read it you can forget half and still succeed! That's why it's good news.

Flash words and flash sentences Read about these building blocks in the **Flash card** section on page 80. Then use them!

Learn by heart Obligatory! Memorizing puts you on the fast track to speaking in full sentences.

Let's speak Italian *You* will be doing the talking – in Italian.

Spot the keys Listen to rapid Italian and make sense of it.

Say it simply Learn how to use plain, **Instant Italian** to say what you want to say. Don't be shy!

Test your progress Mark your own test and be amazed by the result.

Answers This is where you'll find the answers to the exercises.

▶ This icon asks you to switch on the recording.

Pronunciation If you don't know about it and don't have the recording go straight to page 16. You need to know about pronunciation before you can start Week 1.

Progress chart Enter your score each week and monitor your progress. Are you going for *very good* or *outstanding*?

Certificate It's on the last page. In six weeks it will have your name on it!

Since **Instant Italian** was first published the euro has become Italy's official currency. Occasionally – as in this book and the recording that goes with it – you will still hear people using *lire*.

progress chart

At the end of each week record your test score on the progress chart below.

At the end of the course throw out your worst result – anybody can have a bad week – and add up your *five* best weekly scores. Divide the total by five to get your average score and overall course result.

Write your result – *outstanding*, *excellent*, *very good* or *good* – on your **Certificate**. If you scored more than 80% enlarge it and frame it!

Progress chart

90–100%							*outstanding*
80–90%							*excellent*
70–80%							*very good*
60–70%							*good*
Weeks	1	2	3	4	5	6	

Total of five best weeks =

divided by five =

Your final result ______ %

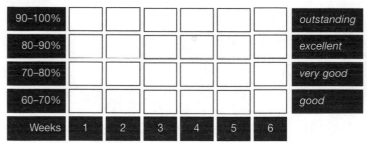

01 week one

Study for 35 minutes – or a little longer if you can!

Day zero

- Read **Read this first!**
- Now read **How this book works.**

Day one

- Read **In the aeroplane**.
- Listen to/Read **In aereo**.
- Listen to/Read the **New words**, then learn some of them.

Day two

- Repeat **In aereo** and the **New words**.
- Listen to/Read **Pronunciation**.
- Learn more **New words**.
- Use the **Flash words** to help you.

Day three

- Learn all the **New words** until you know them well.
- Read and learn the **Good news grammar**.

Day four

- Cut out and learn the **Flash sentences**.
- Listen to/Read **Learn by heart**.

Day five

- Listen to/Read **Let's speak Italian**.
- Revise! Tomorrow you'll be testing your progress.

Day six

- Translate **Test your progress**.

Day seven is your day off!

In the aeroplane

Tom and Kate Walker are on their way to Italy. They are boarding flight QI 915 to Florence via Milan and squeeze past Gino Pavarotti.

Tom Excuse me, we have the seats 9a and 9b.

Gino Yes, sure, one moment please.

Tom Good day, we are Tom and Kate Walker.

Gino Good morning, I am Pavarotti.

Tom Luciano Pavarotti?

Gino No, unfortunately. I am Gino Pavarotti.

Tom We are going to Florence. Also you?

Gino No, I am going to Milan. I am from Verona.

Tom I was in Verona in April. Verona is very beautiful. I was in Verona for my company.

Gino What do you do?

Tom I work with computers.

Gino And you, Mrs Walker? What do you do? Where do you work?

Kate I worked in a school for three years. Now I work at the Rover.

Gino Are you from London?

Kate No, we are from Manchester. We were one year in New York and two years in London. Now we are in Birmingham.

Gino I worked for five years at the Fiat. Now I work at the Bank of Italy.

Tom How is the work at the bank? Good?

Gino The work is boring. I work too much but I need a lot of money. I have a big house, a Ferrari and four children. My wife is American. She has a girlfriend in Florida and telephones always. It costs a lot.

Kate Now we are in holiday. Also you?

Gino No, unfortunately. Not we are in holiday now. We are in holiday in August. We are going to Portofino but without children. We have a house there – and not it has the telephone!

In aereo

Tom and Kate Walker are on their way to Italy. They are boarding flight QI 915 to Firenze via Milano and squeeze past Gino Pavarotti.

Tom	Scusi, abbiamo i posti nove a e nove b.
Gino	Sì, certo, un momento per favore.
Tom	Buongiorno, siamo Tom e Kate Walker.
Gino	Buongiorno, sono Pavarotti.
Tom	Luciano Pavarotti?
Gino	No purtroppo. Sono Gino Pavarotti.
Tom	Andiamo a Firenze. Anche Lei?
Gino	No, vado a Milano. Sono di Verona.
Tom	Sono stato a Verona in aprile. Verona è molto bella. Sono stato a Verona per la mia ditta.
Gino	Che cosa fa?
Tom	Lavoro con computers.
Gino	E Lei, Signora Walker? Cosa fa? Dove lavora?
Kate	Ho lavorato in una scuola per tre anni. Adesso lavoro alla Rover.
Gino	È di Londra?
Kate	No, siamo di Manchester. Siamo stati un anno a New York e due anni a Londra. Adesso siamo a Birmingham.
Gino	Io ho lavorato per cinque anni alla Fiat. Adesso lavoro alla Banca d'Italia.
Tom	Com'è il lavoro alla banca? Buono?
Gino	Il lavoro è noioso. Lavoro troppo ma ho bisogno di molti soldi. Ho una casa grande, una Ferrari e quattro bambini. Mia moglie è americana. Ha un'amica in Florida e telefona sempre. Costa molto.
Kate	Adesso siamo in vacanza. Anche Lei?
Gino	No purtroppo. Non siamo in vacanza adesso. Siamo in vacanza in agosto. Andiamo a Portofino ma senza bambini. Abbiamo una casa là – e non ha il telefono!

New words

Cover up the Italian words, then say them OUT LOUD.

in aereo *in the aeroplane*
scusi *excuse me*
abbiamo *we have*
il, la, i, le, l', gli *the*
posti *seats, places*
nove *nine*
a, b (pronounced **uh, bee**)
e *and*
sì *yes*
certo *sure, certain*
un momento *a moment*
per favore *please*
buongiorno *good day, good morning, hello*
siamo *we are*
sono *I am*
no *no*
purtroppo *unfortunately*
andiamo *we go, we are going*
a *to, at*
anche *also, too*
Lei *you*
vado *I go, am going*
di *from, of*
sono stato/a *I have been, I was*
aprile *April*
è *is he/she/it…? it is, you are*
molto *very, much, a lot*
bello/a *beautiful*
per *for*
il mio, la mia *my*
ditta *firm*
che, che cosa, cosa *what*
fa *you do/do you do?*
lavoro *I work, I am working*
con *with*
Signora *Mrs, woman*
dove? *where?*
lavora *you work/he/she/ it works*
ho; ho lavorato *I have; I have worked, I worked*
un, una, un' *a*
scuola *school*
tre *three*
anno, anni *year, years*
adesso *now*
al, alla *at, at the*
siamo stati *we have been, we were*
due *two*
io *I* (only use to emphasize)
cinque *five*
la Banca d'Italia *The Bank of Italy*
come *how*
com'è (come è) *how is…?*
il lavoro *the work*
buono/a *good*
noioso/a *boring*
troppo *too much*
ma *but*
ho bisogno (di) *I need*
molti soldi *a lot of money*
casa *house*
grande *big*
quattro *four*
bambino/i *child, children*
moglie *wife*
americana *American*
ha *he/she/it has/ you have*
amica *girlfriend*
telefona *she/he telephones*
sempre *always*
costa *it costs*
in vacanza *on holiday*
agosto *August*

senza *without*
là *there*
non *not*
il telefono *the telephone*

TOTAL NEW WORDS: 76
...only 303 words to go!

Some easy extras

These are all very similar to the English!

i mesi (the months)

gennaio, febbraio, marzo, aprile, maggio, giugno, luglio, agosto, settembre, ottobre, novembre, dicembre

i numeri (the numbers)

zero,	uno,	due,	tre,	quattro,	cinque,	sei,	sette,	otto,	nove,	dieci
0	1	2	3	4	5	6	7	8	9	10

More greetings

buona sera *good evening*, **buona notte** *good night*, **ciao** *hello/ goodbye*

Essential verbs for every day: 'to have' and 'to be'

In a couple of days you'll be reading about **verbs** in **Good news grammar**. Then on Day 3 spend ten minutes on these two verbs. I have put them into 'gift boxes' for you so you can't ignore them! But don't learn them today. Don't let's overdo it!

essere	*to be*	
(io)	sono	*I am*
(Lei)	è	*you are*
(lui)	è	*he/it is*
(lei)	è	*she/it is*
(noi)	siamo	*we are*
(loro)	sono	*they are*

avere	*to have*
ho	*I have*
ha	*you have*
ha	*he/it has*
ha	*she/it has*
abbiamo	*we have*
hanno	*they have*

Pronunciation

The Italian language is beautiful, so drop all inhibitions and try to speak Italian rather than English with the words changed!

If Italian pronunciation is new to you please buy the recording. But if you are good at languages, or want a refresher, here are the rules:

First the vowels

The English word in brackets gives you an example of the sound. Say the sound and the Italian examples OUT LOUD.

a	(*pasta*)	vado, f**a**, c**a**sa, gr**a**nde
e	(*yes*)	per, sempre, bella
i	(*field*)	il, si, amica, arrivederci
o	(*not*)	no, non, sono, momento
u	(*June*)	scusi, un, una, purtroppo

When you come across two vowels next to each other, as in **buono**, or andiamo, say each one separately: **bu – o –** no, andi **– a –** mo

Consonants

There are only two which could be confusing: **c** and **g**. Each of these comes in a 'hard' and 'soft' variety, so you need to know when it is a hard sound and when it is soft.

Hard c:	This sounds like the **c** in **c**offee.
c, ch	Either of these two produce the 'hard' sound. **Examples:** casa, cosa, scusi, **ch**e, **ch**ilo (*kilo*)
Soft c:	This sounds like the **ch** in **ch**ocolate.
(c before **e**) (c before **i**)	Either of these two produces a 'soft' sound. **Examples:** certo, cinque
Note: **cia**	Soft **c**, but the **i** is not pronounced. **C**(i)ao! Luc(i)ano
Hard g:	This sounds like the **g** in **g**ood.
g, gh	Either of these two produces a 'hard' sound. **Examples:** golf, **g**rande, spa**gh**etti, In**gh**ilterra (*England*)
Soft g:	This sounds like the **j** in **j**et.
(**g** before **e**) (**g** before **i**) **gia, gio, giu**	Either of these two produces a 'soft' sound. **Examples:** Gino, Genova, via**gg**i Soft **g**, but the **i** is not pronounced. **Examples: g**(i)allo (*yellow*), **g**(i)orno, **G**(i)useppe
h	This is always silent: **ho, ha**: say **o** and **a**!
gn	This sounds like the **ny** in ca**ny**on. **Example:** biso**gn**o (say: 'bisonyo')

(sc before **e**)	These two sound like **sh** in **ship**
(sc before **i**)	**Example:** scena (*scene*), sci (*ski*)
Doubles:	Try to stretch these. Pretend there are four of them!
gg, ll, nn, etc.	bello, a**nn**o, ma**mm**a
gl	This sounds like the **ly** in the misspelt word milyon (*million*): mo**gl**ie (say 'mol-ye') **gl**i (say 'lyee')
z	This sounds like the **z** in **z**ombie – but pretend there is a **d** in front of the **z**. (say: dzombie): agen**z**ia, vacan**z**e

Roll your r's!

Note that the Italian '**r**' always has a clear rolled sound, unlike English.

favo**r**e, t**r**oppo, signo**r**a, Inglate**rr**a

Which syllable to stress

You usually stress the last but one part of the word:

scu-si, ab-bi-**a**-mo, **pos**-ti, mo-**men**-to

But as always there are exceptions – sorry!

te-**le**-fo-na, **cre**-di-to

There is a written accent when the stress falls on the last vowel:

caff**è** (*coffee*), perch**é** (*because*), luned**ì** (*Monday*)

and to differentiate between two words spelt the same way: si (*if*), sì (*yes*). If you want to hear 'the real thing', treat yourself to the recording.

Learn by heart

Don't be tempted to skip this exercise because it reminds you of school... If you want to speak, not stumble, saying a few lines by heart does the trick.

Learn **Buongiorno** by heart after you have filled in the gaps with your personal, or any other information. Say **Buongiorno** aloud and fairly fast. Can you beat 40 seconds?

Buongiorno!

Buongiorno, sono ....(*name*).
Sono di ....(*place*).
Sono stato/a* a....................(*place*) in..............................(*month*).
Ho lavorato alla..(*firm*) per due anni.
Adesso lavoro alla...(*firm*).
Ho una casa grande a.................................(*place*) e costa molto.
In agosto andiamo a..(*place*).
Com'è Firenze in aprile? bella?

*__stato__ *if you are male*, **stata** *if you are female*

Good news grammar

This is the **Good News** part of each week. Remember I promised: No Ghastly Grammar! I simply explain the differences between English and Italian. This will help you to speak Italian **instantly!**

1 Names of things – nouns

There are two kinds of nouns in Italian: masculine and feminine. You can tell which is which by the word **il** or **la** (*the*), or **un** or **una** (*a* or *one*) in front of the word. You can also tell by the ending of the noun.

Most masculine nouns end in **-o: il lavoro, il telefono, un momento.**

Most feminine nouns end in **-a: la ditta, una casa**. The adjective describing the noun also ends in **-o** or **-a**. So the *good work* or *house* becomes: **il lavoro buono** or **una casa buona.**

When you talk about more than one thing (plural) the **il** and **la** change into **i** and **le**. And to complete the jigsaw, all words ending in **-o** and **-a** end in **-i** and **-e** in the plural.

...**i** posti buoni *the good seats* **le** case belle *the beautiful houses*

This may sound complicated, but it is really easy, and you'll learn it without even noticing. If you get muddled and say 'il casa bello' or 'le vacanze buoni', Italians will still understand you perfectly!

Some nouns end in **-e**, so you can't tell what they are. In the **New words** they have **il** or **la** in front of them so you'll know.

The plural of **-e** is **-i**: **cane** → **cani** (*dog* → *dogs*).

2 Doing things – verbs

Unlike the English the Italians do not use *I*, *you*, *he*, *she*, *it*, *we*, or *they*, to identify who is doing something unless they wish to clarify or stress it. So the only way you can tell who is doing something is by the verb itself. Each person has his or her own verb form or verb ending, but sometimes a verb or an ending is shared. This could lead to some confusion, but amazingly it usually works out all right. There are a few verbs which you'll use every day. I have put the first two in a box on page 15. Learn them now, it won't take long!

3 Asking questions

This is very easy. In Italian there is no difference between *Rome is beautiful.* and *Is Rome beautiful?* **Roma è bella. Roma è bella?**
Costa molto. *It costs a lot.* **Costa molto?** *Does it cost a lot?*

Just use your voice to turn a statement into a question.

Let's speak Italian

Here are ten English sentences. Read each sentence and say it in Italian – OUT LOUD! If you have the recording, listen to check your answers to **Let's speak Italian**.

1 Are you from London?
2 Yes, I am from London.
3 I am on holiday in August.
4 We are going to Como.
5 I was in Milan for my firm.
6 Do you have a Ferrari?
7 No, unfortunately.
8 We have a house in Rome.
9 How is the job with Fiat, good?
10 No, it is boring, but I need a lot of money.

Well, how many did you get right? If you are not happy do it again.

Here are some questions in Italian. Answer these in Italian. Start every answer with **sì** and talk about yourself.

11 È di Manchester?
12 Ha una casa a Londra?
13 Andiamo a Firenze. Anche Lei?
14 Lavora in una ditta a Torino?
15 Il lavoro è buono?

Now tell someone in Italian…

16 … that you have two children.
17 … that you have been in Torino.
18 … that you have a Fiat Uno.
19 … that you need a girlfriend.
20 … that Birmingham is boring in November.

Answers

1 È di Londra?
2 Sì, sono di Londra.
3 Sono in vacanza in agosto.
4 Andiamo a Como.
5 Sono stato (or stata) a Milano per la mia ditta.
6 Ha una Ferrari?
7 No purtroppo.
8 Abbiamo una casa a Roma.
9 Com'è il lavoro alla Fiat, buono?
10 No, è noioso, ma ho bisogno di molti soldi.
11 Sì, sono di Manchester.
12 Sì, ho una casa a Londra.
13 Sì, vado a Firenze.
14 Sì, lavoro in una ditta a Torino.
15 Sì, il lavoro è buono.
16 Ho due bambini.
17 Sono stato/stata a Torino.
18 Ho una Fiat Uno.
19 Ho bisogno di una amica.
20 Birmingham è noiosa in novembre.

Well, what was your score? For 20/20 take a triple gold star!

Test your progress

This is your only written exercise. You'll be amazed how easy it is! Translate the 20 sentences without looking at the previous pages.

1 Good morning, we are Helen and Jane.
2 I am from Rome, you too?
3 Where do you work now?
4 I was in Milan in October.
5 My girlfriend is in Italy for one year.
6 We always go to Pisa in June.
7 I worked at Fiat in May.
8 What do you do in London?
9 I work in a school but without money.
10 The big house in Bologna is for the children.
11 One moment please, where is Luigi?
12 Does the house have a telephone? No, unfortunately (not).
13 Does a Ferrari cost a lot? Yes, sure, it costs too much.
14 How is the work in Italy, good?
15 Mario has a friend in an American firm.
16 We were in Como for three days.
17 We have (the) good seats in (the) aeroplane.
18 I always have (the) boring holidays.
19 I need a beautiful wife, a Lamborghini and a lot of money...
20 He telephones now with a firm in London.

When you have finished, look up the answers on page 74 and mark your work. Then enter your result on the **Progress chart** on page 9. If your score is higher than 80% you'll have done very well indeed!

02 week two

35 minutes a day – but a little extra will step up your progress!

Day one

- Read **In Tuscany**.
- Listen to/Read **In Toscana**.
- Listen to/Read the **New words**. Learn 20 easy ones.

Day two

- Repeat **In Toscana** and the **New words**.
- Go over **Pronunciation**, if you need to.
- Learn the harder **New words**.
- Use the **Flash words** to help you.

Day three

- Learn all the **New words** until you know them well.
- Read and learn the **Good news grammar**.

Day four

- Cut out and learn the ten **Flash sentences**.
- Have a first go at **Let's speak Italian**.

Day five

- Listen to/Read **Let's speak Italian**.
- Listen to/Read **Learn by heart**.

Day six

- Go over **Non ho molti soldi...**
- Translate **Test your progress**.

Day seven is a study-free day!

In Tuscany

In Florence Tom and Kate hire a car and drive through Tuscany. They speak to Carla Rossi of 'Pensione Rossi' and later to Paolo, the waiter.

Kate Good day. Do you have a room double for one night and not too expensive?

Carla Yes, we have a room a little small with bath and shower. But the shower is broken. Perhaps my husband it can repair.

Tom Where is the room?

Carla It is here on the left. Is it enough big?

Tom It is a little small but not it is bad. How much does it cost?

Carla Only 70.000 lire for two, but no cards of credit! The breakfast is from eight to nine and half.

Tom All right, it we take. But can we make breakfast at eight less a quarter? Tomorrow at eight and a quarter we would like to go to Portofino.

Kate And excuse me, where can we drink something? Is there a bar here?

Carla There are two bars at five minutes from here. Not it is difficult. 30 metres on the right and then always straight on.

(In the bar)

Paolo What would you like?

Kate We would like a coffee and a tea with milk.

Paolo Would you like also something to eat?

Tom What is there?

Paolo We have cake of apples or rolls.

Kate Two rolls with ham, please.

Tom The ham not is good.

Kate The mine is very good.

Tom The table is too small.

Kate But the toilets are big and very clean.

Tom The tea is cold.

Kate But the waiter is very handsome.

Tom Waiter, the bill please!

Paolo 13,000 lire, please.

In Toscana

In Firenze Tom and Kate hire a car and drive through Toscana. They speak to Carla Rossi of 'Pensione Rossi' and later to Paolo, the 'cameriere'.

Kate Buongiorno, ha una camera doppia per una notte e non troppo cara?

Carla Sì, abbiamo una camera un po' piccola con bagno e doccia. Però la doccia è rotta. Forse mio marito la può riparare.

Tom Dov'è la camera?

Carla È qui a sinistra. È abbastanza grande?

Tom È un po' piccola ma non è male. Quanto costa?

Carla Solo settanta mila lire per due, però niente carte di credito! La colazione è dalle otto alle nove e mezza.

Tom Va bene, la prendiamo. Però possiamo fare colazione alle otto meno un quarto? Domani alle otto e un quarto vorremmo andare a Portofino.

Kate E scusi, dove possiamo bere qualcosa? C'è un bar qui?

Carla Ci sono due bar a cinque minuti da qui. Non è difficile. Trenta metri a destra e poi sempre diritto.

(Nel bar)

Paolo Cosa desiderano?

Kate Vorremmo un caffè e un tè con latte.

Paolo Desiderano anche qualcosa da mangiare?

Tom Che cosa c'è?

Paolo Abbiamo della torta di mele o dei panini.

Kate Due panini con prosciutto per favore.

Tom Il prosciutto non è buono.

Kate Il mio è molto buono.

Tom La tavola è troppo piccola.

Kate Però i servizi sono grandi e molto puliti.

Tom Il tè è freddo.

Kate Ma il cameriere è molto bello.

Tom Cameriere, il conto per favore!

Paolo Tredicimila lire per favore.

New words

Learning words the traditional way can be boring. If you enjoyed the flash cards why not make your own for the rest of the words. Always say the words OUT LOUD. It's the fast track to speaking!

camera *room*
doppio/a *double*
la notte *the night*
caro/a *expensive, dear*
un po', un pochino *a little, a very little*
piccolo, piccola *small*
bagno *bath*
però *but*
doccia *shower*
rotto/a *broken*
forse *perhaps*
marito *husband*
lo, la (by itself) *it, him, her*
può *he/she/it/you can* (formal)
riparare *(to) repair*
qui *here*
a sinistra *on (the) left*
abbastanza *enough*
male *bad*
quanto/a *how much...?*
solo *only*
settanta mila *70,000*
lire *Italian currency*
niente *no, nothing, not anything*
carta di credito *credit card*
la prima colazione *the breakfast*
da – a *from – to/until*
mezzo, mezza *half*
va bene *all right, OK*
prendiamo *we'll take*
possiamo *we can*
fare colazione *to have breakfast*
meno *less/before (with time)*
un quarto *a quarter*
domani *tomorrow*
vorremmo *we would like*
andare *(to) go*
bere *(to) drink*
qualcosa *something*
c'è *there is*
ci sono *there are*
minuto, minuti *minute, minutes*
difficile *difficult*
(a) destra *(on the) right*
poi *then*
diritto *straight on*
nel bar *in the bar*
il cameriere *the waiter*
cosa desiderano? *what would you like?* (formal)
(il) caffè *coffee*
il tè *tea*
il latte *the milk*
da mangiare *(something to) eat*
torta di mele *apple cake (cake of apples)*
o *or*
panino, panini *roll, rolls*
prosciutto *ham*
tavola *table*
i servizi *the toilets*
pulito/a *clean*
freddo/a *cold*
conto *bill*
tredicimila *13,000*

TOTAL NEW WORDS: 63
...only 240 to go!

Some useful extras

i numeri (numbers)

11 **undici**	19 **diciannove**	60 **sessanta**
12 **dodici**	20 **venti**	70 **settanta**
13 **tredici**	21 **ventuno**	80 **ottanta**
14 **quattordici**	22 **ventidue**	90 **novanta**
15 **quindici**	23 **ventitrè**	100 **cento**
16 **sedici**	30 **trenta**	200 **due cento**
17 **diciassette**	40 **quaranta**	1,000 **mile**
18 **diciotto**	50 **cinquanta**	

il tempo (time)

a che ora?	*at what time?*	**un' ora**	*an hour*
alle cinque	*at five o'clock*	**un giorno**	*a day*
è l'una	*it is one o'clock*	**una settimana**	*a week*
sono le due	*it is two o'clock*	**un mese**	*a month*
un minuto	*a minute*	**un anno**	*a year*

half past = and half	**e mezzo**
quarter past = and a quarter	**e un quarto**
quarter to = less a quarter	**meno un quarto**

Good news grammar

1 *I, you, he, she, we, they*

In Italian these are: **io, Lei** or **tu, lui, lei, noi, loro**. But as you know they are only used for emphasis: *I do this*, *you did that*. **Lei** (*you*), as opposed to **lei** (*she*), takes a capital **L. Lei** is the formal and polite way of saying *you*. When in Italy and speaking **Instant Italian** use **Lei. Tu** is for family and friends, and requires a great deal more extra grammar. Next year!

2 Saying *non* (not)

Did you notice what happened to 'not' when Signor Pavarotti said:

> **Non** abbiamo le vacanze adesso. *Not we have the holidays now.*

The 'not' moved in front of the verb. It does this all the time:

> Il lavoro è buono. Il lavoro **non** è buono *The work **not** is good.*

3 Verbs – again

This week's Good news: two more everyday verbs – *can* and *go* – in 'gift boxes', for easy learning. You'll need only a few minutes this time, because there is a bit of a pattern to each verb:

I usually ends in -o: **sono, ho, vado, lavoro**
you, he, she and *it* end in -e or -a: **è, ha, va, lavora,** but **può** (sorry)
we usually ends in **-iamo**: **andiamo, abbiamo, possiamo, prendiamo**
they usually ends in **-ono** or **-an(n)o**: **sono, possono, hanno, vanno**
Dead simple, isn't it?

Now learn **andare** and **potere**. Spend five minutes on each.

andare	*(to) go*
vado	*I go*
va	*you go*
	he, she, it goes
andiamo	*we go*
vanno	*they go*

potere	*can*
posso	*I can*
può	*you can*
	he, she, it can
possiamo	*we can*
possono	*they can*

More good news: there's a complete summary of verbs in Week 6 **Good news grammar** – if you get confused. Have a sneak preview! You'll know most of these in four weeks time!

4 *C'è/ci sono*: there is – is there?/there are – are there?

You will use this a lot, especially when asking questions.

C'è un bar qui. Che cosa **c'è**? Ci **sono** servizi?
C'è un cameriere molto bello?... Sì, sì...!

5 No collisions!

When two, usually identical vowels meet, like **a+a** or **e+e**, one is dropped:

un'amica (not una amica), **dov'è** (not dove è), **c'è** (not ce è)
More smooth talk!

6 *della, dei*

This is just a way of saying *some* cake or *some* rolls. Nothing too serious.

Let's speak Italian

Now let's practise what you have learned. Here are ten English sentences for you to say in Italian OUT LOUD! After each sentence check to see if you got it right. If you didn't tick all ten, do the exercise again.

1 We would like a room.
2 At what time is there breakfast?
3 The telephone is broken.
4 How much is (costs) the room?
5 Where is the bar, on the right or on the left?
6 Is there something to eat?
7 All right, we take it.
8 Can we go to Florence?
9 We would like to go at half past two.
10 Excuse me, the bill please.

Now answer the Italian. Use **Sì** and speak about yourself.

11 Va alle otto e mezza?
12 Può mangiare un panino?
13 Ha una carta di credito?

Now answer with **No** and speak for yourself and a friend:

14 Ha una tavola per quattro?
15 Può riparare la Rover?
16 Va a Roma domani?

And now answer freely. Your answers may differ from mine but be correct.

17 Dov'è la pensione Rossi?
18 Com'è la camera?
19 Dove c'è un bar qui?
20 A che ora va a Milano Gina?

Answers

1 Vorremmo una camera.
2 A che ora c'è la prima colazione?
3 Il telefono è rotto.
4 Quanto costa la camera?
5 Dov'è il bar, a destra o a sinistra?
6 C'è qualcosa da manigiare?
7 Va bene, lo (*or* la) prendiamo.
8 Possiamo andare a Firenze?
9 Vorremmo andare alle due e mezza.
10 Scusi, il conto per favore.
11 Sì, vado alle otto e mezza.
12 Sì, posso mangiare un panino.
13 Sì, ho una carta di credito.
14 No, non abbiamo una tavola per quattro.
15 No, non possiamo riparare la Rover (*or* ripararla).
16 No, domani non andiamo a Roma.
17 La pensione Rossi è in Toscana.
18 La camera è un po' piccola ma non è male.
19 C'è un bar a dieci minuti da qui, a sinistra e poi sempre diritto.
20 (Gina) Va a Milano alle otto.

Did you get more than half right the first time? Have a gold star!

Learn by heart

Learn the seven lines **Non ho molti soldi però...** by **Heart**. Try to say them with a bit of 'drama' in 45–60 seconds! Choose one of these to fill the gap:

mio marito, mia moglie, il mio amico, la mia amica.

Non ho molti soldi però...
Non ho molti soldi però vorrei* andare in Italia con...
Vorremmo andare a Portofino con la Rover.
È molto bello in aprile.
La pensione Rossi non è molto cara.
Quanto costa? Solo settanta mila lire la notte.
Lo posso fare?
No. C'è sempre troppo lavoro nella mia ditta, e – la Rover è rotta!
***vorrei**: *I would like to*

Test your progress

Translate in writing. What do you remember without checking back?

1 Where is there a telephone?
2 Excuse me, we only have a (the) credit card.
3 Can we eat at seven tomorrow?
4 Do you have a big enough table? We are (in) five.
5 The small rooms do not have a (the) bath.
6 We would like to eat ham and melon. (**melone**)
7 We can go from six to quarter to seven.
8 Where can we drink something?
9 We have been in the (**al**) bar from nine to half past ten.
10 All right, we take the Fiat for a day.
11 How much does the breakfast cost? Only 6,000 lire.
12 Let's go and (to) repair the computer. It is broken.
13 How is the milk? Can the child drink it?
14 Where are the toilets, on the right or on the left?
15 Can I go to Hollywood – without my husband?
16 A coffee, please – nothing for you?
17 Where is (the) Signora Rossi? Perhaps in the (**nel**) bar?
18 Five thousand lire for a cold tea – it is a little expensive!
19 I have been in Tuscany in February. It is not bad.
20 There are 300 bars here, one at a hundred metres from here.

The answers are on page 75. The **Progress chart** awaits your score!

03 week three

Study for 35 minutes a day – but there are no penalties for doing more!

Day one

- Read **We are going shopping.**
- Listen to/Read **Andiamo a fare spese.**
- Read the **New words**, then learn some of them.

Day two

- Repeat **Andiamo a fare spese** and the **New words**.
- Learn all the **New words**. Use the **Flash cards!**

Day three

- Test yourself on all the **New words** – boring, boring, but you are over halfway already!
- Learn the **Good news grammar**.

Day four

- Cut out and learn the **Flash sentences**.
- Listen to/Read **Learn by heart**.

Day five

- Listen to/Read **Let's speak Italian**.
- Listen to/Read **Spot the keys**.

Day six

- Have a quick look at the **New words** from Weeks 1–3. You now know 216 words! ... well, more or less.
- Translate **Test your progress**.

Day seven is your day off!

Let's go shopping

Tom and Kate are in La Spezia near Portofino. They have rented a holiday appartment for a week. Kate plans to do some shopping…

Kate Today we must do the shopping. Let's go into the centre with the bus.

Tom But there is bad weather, it makes cold and there is a lot of sport in television ... the golf at two and half ...

Kate I am sorry, but we must first go to the cash dispenser and into post office or tobacconist for the stamps ... then into chemist's and into dry cleaner's.

Tom In that case no golf ... perhaps the football at four and a quarter ... is it all?

Kate No, we have to go in a big store to buy a suitcase new. Then I have to go to the supermarket and to the hairdresser's. And afterwards I would like to buy some shoes.

Tom Bother...! Until when are open the shops?

Kate Until seven and half, I believe.

Tom Therefore no football,... perhaps the tennis at eight.

(Later)

Kate Hello Tom, here is the shopping: 200 grams of ham, a piece of cheese, half a kilo of apples, two kilos of potatoes, a mozzarella, sugar, bread, butter, some eggs, six beers and a bottle of wine. I have bought too much.

Tom It doesn't matter. Yesterday not we have eaten much. And what is there in the bag big? Something for me?

Kate Well,... near to the UPIM there was a shop small and I have seen some shoes which were of my size. Not are they beautiful? White and blue. The sales assistant was very nice and handsome like Tom Cruise.

Tom Who is Tom Cruise? And how much cost the shoes?

Kate They were a very little expensive... but they cost the same in England... 300,000 lire.

Tom What? My wife is crazy!

Kate But this T-shirt for the golf was very cheap. Size 42, only 25,000 lire. Here is a newspaper English ... and now not is there the tennis in television?

Andiamo a fare spese

Tom and Kate are in La Spezia near Portofino. They have rented a holiday appartment for a week. Kate plans to do some shopping…

Kate Oggi dobbiamo fare spese. Andiamo in centro con l'autobus.

Tom Ma c'è brutto tempo, fa freddo e c'è molto sport in televisione … il golf alle due e mezza…

Kate Mi dispiace ma dobbiamo prima passare dal Bankomat e in posta o dal tabaccaio per i francobolli … poi in farmacia e in tintoria.

Tom Dunque niente golf … forse il calcio alle quattro e un quarto … è tutto?

Kate No, dobbiamo andare in un grande magazzino per comprare una valigia nuova. Poi devo passare dal supermercato e dal parrucchiere. E dopo vorrei comprare delle scarpe.

Tom Uffa...! Fino a quando sono aperti i negozi?

Kate Fino alle sette e mezza, credo.

Tom Dunque niente calcio … forse il tennis alle otto.

(Più tardi)

Kate Ciao, Tom, ecco la spesa: 200 grammi di prosciutto, un pezzo di formaggio, mezzo chilo di mele, due chili di patate, una mozzarella, zucchero, pane, burro, qualche uovo, sei birre e una bottiglia di vino. Ho comprato troppo.

Tom Non importa. Ieri non abbiamo mangiato molto. E cosa c'è nella borsa grande? Qualcosa per me?

Kate Beh … Vicino alla UPIM c'era un negozio piccolo e ho visto delle scarpe che erano del mio numero. Non sono belle? Bianche e blu. Il commesso era molto simpatico e bello come Tom Cruise.

Tom Chi è Tom Cruise? E quanto costano le scarpe?

Kate Erano un pochino care … ma costano lo stesso in Inghilterra … 300,000 lire.

Tom Cosa? Mia moglie è pazza!

Kate Però questa T-shirt per il golf era molto conveniente. Taglia 42, solo 25,000 lire. Ecco un giornale inglese … e adesso non c'è il tennis in televisione?

New words

Learn the **New words** in half the time using the flash cards. There are 18 to start you off. Get a friend to make the rest!

fare spese *to do (the) shopping*
oggi *today*
dobbiamo *we must*
centro *centre*
autobus *bus*
brutto *bad, ugly*
tempo *weather* (also *time*)
fa freddo *it is cold* (used with weather)
la televisione *the TV*
mi dispiace *I am sorry*
prima *first*
passare (da) *pass, call on, go (to)*
il Bankomat *name of cash dispenser*
posta *post office*
il tabaccaio *the tobacconist's* (sells stamps)
francobolli *stamps*
farmacia *chemist's pharmacy*
tintoria *dry cleaner's*
dunque *therefore, in that case*
calcio *football*
tutto *all*
grande magazzino *department store*
comprare *(to) buy*
valigia *suitcase*
nuovo/a *new*
supermercato *supermarket*
il parrucchiere *the hairdresser's*
dopo *after, afterwards*
vorrei *I would like*
negozio, negozi *shop, shops*
le scarpe *the shoes*
uffa! something you say when you are fed up, e.g. *bother, damn*
fino a *until*
quando *when*
aperto *open*
credo *I think, believe*
più tardi *later*
ecco *here, here is/here are*
la spesa *the shopping*
grammi *grams*
pezzo *piece*
formaggio *cheese*
chilo *kilo*
patate *potatoes*
zucchero *sugar*
il pane *bread*
burro *butter*
qualche *some*
uovo, uova *egg, eggs*
birra, birre *beer, beers*
bottiglia *bottle*
vino *wine*
ho comprato *I bought, have bought*
non importa *no problem, it doesn't matter*
ieri *yesterday*
abbiamo mangiato *we ate, have eaten*
borsa *bag*
me, mi *me*
beh... *well...*
vicino, vicino a *near, near to*
la UPIM *well-known Italian chain store*
era/erano *was/were*
ho visto *I have seen*
bianco *white*
blu *blue*
commesso/a *sales assistant*
simpatico/a *nice*
chi *who*

costano *they cost*
lo stesso *the same*
Inghilterra *England*
pazzo/a *crazy*
questo/a *this*
conveniente *cheap*
taglia *size*
il giornale *the newspaper*
inglese *English*

TOTAL NEW WORDS: 77
...only 163 words to go!

Some easy extras: *i colori* (colours)

bianco *white*
nero *black*
rosso *red*
blu *blue*
verde *green*
giallo *yellow*
marrone *brown*
grigio *grey*
arancione *orange*
rosa *pink*

Good news grammar

1 Doing more things with verbs: the past

Imagine you are getting married today! You would say 'I do.' If it happened yesterday, you would say 'I did' or 'I have done it.' To talk about something that happened before or in the past in Italian, you use *have* – which you know already – plus a slightly changed main verb.

So, **mangiare** becomes **mangiato** and **comprare** becomes **comprato**.

I bought, or *I have bought*	ho compr**ato**
you bought, or *you have bought* / *he/she/it bought,* or *has bought*	ha compr**ato**
we bought, or *we have bought*	abbiamo compr**ato**
they bought, or *they have bought*	hanno compr**ato**

And how about **mangiare?** How would you say: *We ate?* **Abbiamo mangiato!** Easy! ...and **riparare?** How would you ask *Have you repaired?* **Ha riparato? Sì!**

Unfortunately not all verbs change to **-ato**. Here are a couple of 'rebels'.

essere (*to be*) but **sono stato/a** (*I was, I have been*)
andare (*to go*) but **sono andato/a** (*I went, I have gone*)

As you can see **andare** (*go*) and **essere** (*be*) behave very strangely. Instead of *I **have*** you say *I **am** gone* and *I **am** been.*

Are you gone to Milano?	**È andato a Milano?**
No, I am not gone…	**No, non sono andato.**

No need to panic. By the end of Week 6 these two will be good friends.

2 Joining little words: turning two into one

Italians love their language to be smooth. Little pairs like *to–the*, *of–the* or *from–the* sound too 'staccato' to them so they 'melt' the two words into one. Here are six to give you a feel for them:

a + il = **al**	da + il = **dal**	su + la = **sulla**
di + la = **della**	in + il = **nel**	con + il = **col**

And if you don't 'melt'? No problem. Everyone will understand you.

3 *Passare da/passare in*

Both mean *to go to….*

Passo **dal** Bancomat – *but* passo **in** un grande magazzino.

Don't worry if you use the wrong one – nobody will laugh.

4 *Il mio, la mia, il suo, la sua*

When Italians say *my, your, his,* or *her* they always add *the.*

Il mio cane… **la** sua ditta… Sounds very grand, doesn't it?

Funnily enough, when you talk about your partner you simply say: **mio marito** or **mia moglie.** By the way, if you forget, it doesn't matter!

Learn by heart

Say this dialogue in under one minute and with a lot of expression!

Dobbiamo fare spese…UFFA!

Tom Oggi fa freddo. C'è il calcio in televisione.

Kate Mi dispiace ma dobbiamo fare spese. Non abbiamo niente da mangiare. Dobbiamo prima passare dal Bankomat e dopo dal supermercato.

(più tardi)

Kate Ecco la spesa! Ho comprato molto: prosciutto, formaggio, pane e burro, e – francobolli per l'Inghilterra.

Tom Niente birre? niente vino? niente per me? Uffa!

Let's speak Italian

Over to you! If you have the recording, use it to check your answers. Always answer OUT LOUD! Start with a ten-point warm-up. Say in Italian:

1 Now we must go.
2 I would like to do the shopping.
3 Are the shops open?
4 I am sorry, but it is too expensive.
5 Is there a bus for the centre?
6 We have eaten at 'Mario's'.
7 Can we buy wine in the supermarket?
8 It costs thirty-seven thousand lire.
9 We have been here from three to half past four.
10 Damn, the bottle is broken!

Answer in Italian using **No**. Speak about yourself.

11 Ha bisogno di un Bankomat?
12 Ha visto il calcio in televisione?
13 Ha comprato tutto in farmacia?

Answer in Italian using the words in brackets.

14 Cosa ha comprato? (niente)
15 Quando va al calcio? (oggi, alle due)
16 Fino a che ora è aperto? (fino alle nove)
17 Chi ha mangiato troppo? (noi)
18 Dove ha visto la valigia? (un negozio)
19 Ha comprato qui i francobolli? (no, in posta)
20 Che tempo fa oggi? (brutto, freddo)

Answers

1 Adesso dobbiamo andare.
2 Vorrei fare spese.
3 Sono aperti i negozi?
4 Mi dispiace ma è troppo caro.
5 C'è un autobus per il centro?
6 Abbiamo mangiato 'da Mario'.
7 Possiamo comprare vino nel supermercato?
8 Costa trentasettemila lire.
9 Siamo stati qui dalle tre alle quattro e mezza.
10 Uffa! La bottiglia è rotta!
11 No, non ho bisogno di un Bankomat.
12 No, non ho visto il calcio in televisone.
13 No, non ho comprato tutto in farmacia.
14 Non ho comprato niente.
15 Vado oggi, alle due.
16 È aperto fino alle nove.
17 Noi abbiamo mangiato troppo.
18 Ho visto la valigia in un negozio.
19 No, ho comprato i francobolli in posta.
20 C'è brutto tempo. Fa freddo.

▶ Spot the keys

By now you can say many things in Italian. But what happens if you ask a question and don't understand the answer – hitting you at the speed of an automatic rifle? The smart way is not to panic, but to listen only for the words you know. Any familiar words which you pick up will provide you with **Key words** – clues to what the other person is saying.

If you have the recording, listen to the dialogue. If you don't – read on.

You **Scusi, dov'è la posta per favore?**

An Italian *Èmoltofacile,* **prima sempre diritto**, *finoalprossimoincrocio,* **dove c'è** *quel* **grande magazzino bianco. Poi a sinistra** *c'èunasiloeuna* **tintoria** *epropriovicinoalla* **banca c'è la posta!**

Can you find your way with the key words? I think you'll get there!

Test your progress

Translate in writing. Then check the answers and be amazed!

1 First, I would like to go to the cash dispenser.
2 In this shop the shoes cost too much.
3 Did you see my husband in the pharmacy?
4 We were here until a quarter past ten.
5 We saw the tennis in England, on (in) television.
6 I am sorry, we do not have the same in red in size 44.
7 This shop is not cheap.
8 Who repaired my telephone? You?
9 Here is the department store. But it is not open.
10 Today we did not buy too much. Only bread and half a kilo of butter.
11 I ate everything – eggs, apples, potatoes and a piece of cheese.
12 We must do the shopping. Is this the centre?
13 Yesterday I was in the office until nine o'clock.
14 The English newspapers cost a lot in Italy.
15 Is there a bus? No? It does not matter.
16 He was a very nice sales assistant.
17 What is this? Something for us?
18 Did she buy the bag near here (here near) or at the UPIM?
19 Everything was very expensive. Therefore I did not buy anything.
20 We need three kilos I believe.

Remember to fill in the **Progress chart**. You are now halfway home!

04 week four

Study 35 minutes a day but if you are keen try 40... 45...!

Day one

- Read **We are going to eat.**
- Listen to/Read **Andiamo a mangiare.**
- Read the **New words**. Learn the easy ones.

Day two

- Repeat the dialogue. Learn the harder **New words**.
- Cut out the **Flash words** to help you.

Day three

- Learn all the **New words** until you know them well.
- Read and learn the **Good news grammar**.

Day four

- Cut out and learn the **Flash sentences**.
- Listen to/Read **Learn by heart**.

Day five

- Read **Say it simply**.
- Listen to/Read **Let's speak Italian**.

Day six

- Listen to/Read **Spot the keys**.
- Translate **Test your progress**.

Day seven

Are you keeping your scores above 60%? In that case ... **have a good day off!**

Let's go and eat

Tom and Kate are back in Florence. Bruno Verdi invites them to dinner.

Kate Tom, someone has telephoned. He did not say why. Signor Verdi from Milan. Here is the number.

Tom Ah yes, Bruno Verdi, a good client. His firm is in Milan. I know him well, he is very nice. I have an appointment with him on Thursday. It is an important matter.

Tom *(Telephones)* Hello! Good morning Mr Verdi. I am Tom Walker… Yes, thank you… yes, sure, it is possible… of course… next week, very interesting… no, we have time. Wonderful! No, only two days… ah yes… when? Tonight, at eight… upstairs, by the exit… in front of the door… All right! In that case, until tonight, thank you very much, goodbye.

Kate What are we doing tonight?

Tom We are going to eat with Mr Verdi. In the centre, behind the church. He says that it is a new and very good restaurant. Mr Verdi is in Florence for three days with Edith and Peter Palmer from our company.

Kate I know Edith Palmer. She is boring and believes to know everything. She has a terrible dog. Well... I believe I am sick. A bad cold and pains. I need a doctor.

Tom No, please. One cannot do that. Mr Verdi is very important.

(At the restaurant) Luigi, the head waiter, explains the menu.

Luigi The fish is not on the menu and for dessert today there is tiramisu or some ice cream.

Bruno Mrs Walker, can I help you? Perhaps some pasta and afterwards meat or fish?

Kate A steak with salad please.

Edith A steak, Kate? It is too much red meat.

Bruno And you, Mr Walker, what are you having? And what would you like to drink?

Tom A veal cutlet 'alla Milanese' with chips and vegetables, and a beer, please.

Edith There is a lot of oil in the vegetables, Tom.

→ Page 46

Andiamo a mangiare

Tom and Kate are back in Florence. Bruno Verdi invites them to dinner.

Kate Tom, ha telefonato qualcuno. Non ha detto perché. Il Signor Verdi di Milano. Ecco il numero.

Tom Ah si, Bruno Verdi, un buon cliente. La sua ditta è a Milano. Lo conosco bene, è molto simpatico. Ho un appuntamento con lui giovedì. È una cosa importante.

Tom *(Telefona)* Pronto! Buongiorno Signor Verdi. Sono Tom Walker... Sì, grazie... sì, certo, è possibile... naturalmente... la settimana prossima, molto interessante... no, abbiamo tempo. Benissimo!... No, solo due giorni... ah sì... quando? Stasera, alle otto... su, all' uscita... davanti alla porta... Va bene! Dunque a stasera, grazie mille, arrivederci.

Kate Cosa facciamo stasera?

Tom Andiamo a mangiare con il Signor Verdi. In centro, dietro alla chiesa. Dice che è un ristorante nuovo e molto buono. Il Signor Verdi è a Firenze per tre giorni con Edith e Peter Palmer della nostra ditta.

Kate Conosco Edith Palmer. È noiosa e crede di sapere tutto. Ha un cane terribile. Beh... Credo di essere malata. Un brutto raffreddore e dolori. Ho bisogno del medico...

Tom No per favore! Non si può fare! Il Signor Rossi è molto importante.

(Al ristorante) Luigi, il cameriere, spiega il menù.

Luigi Il pesce non è sul menù e come dessert oggi c'è il tiramisù o del gelato.

Bruno Signora Walker, posso aiutarla? Forse della pasta e dopo carne o pesce?

Kate Una bistecca con insalata per favore.

Edith Una bistecca, Kate? È troppa carne rossa!

Bruno E Lei, Signor Walker, cosa prende? E cosa desidera bere?

Tom Una cotoletta alla milanese con patatine e verdura, e una birra per favore.

Edith C'è molto olio nella verdura, Tom.

→ Page 47

Bruno And you, Mrs Palmer?

Edith I take some chicken and a glass of water, please.

(Later)

Bruno Are we having fruit, or perhaps better – the tiramisu? No? Nothing? Have we finished? A coffee for someone? Nobody? Good, the bill, please.

Edith Mr Verdi, please help me! How does one say 'doggy bag' in Italian? I would like a little meat for my dog.

Kate But Edith, the dog is in England!

New words

qualcuno *someone*
ha detto *he/she/it has said, you said*
perché *why, because*
signor *Mr, gentleman*
il cliente *the client*
il suo, la sua *his/her* (agrees with noun)
conosco *I know*
bene *well, also good!*
appuntamento *appointment*
con lui *with him*
giovedì *Thursday*
una cosa *a matter, a thing*
importante *important*
pronto! *ready* (and what you say when you answer the phone)
grazie, grazie mille *thank you, many (a thousand!) thanks*
certo *sure, certain*
possibile *possible*
naturalmente *of course*
la settimana prossima *next week*
interessante *interesting*
benissimo *very good, excellent*
su *up, upstairs,* also *on*
uscita *exit*
davanti a *in front of, before*
porta *door*
stasera *tonight*
facciamo *we do, make*
dietro a *behind*
chiesa *church*
dice *he/she/it says, you say*
che *that*
il ristorante *the restaurant*
nostro/a *our*
crede *he/she/it believes, you believe*
sapere *(to) know*
il cane *the dog*
terribile *terrible*
malato/a *sick, ill*
un raffreddore *a cold*
dolori *pains*
medico *doctor*
non si può fare *one can't do that, that's not on*
il pesce *the fish*
il menù *the menu*
come *like, as*
gelato *ice cream*
posso *I can*
aiutare *(to) help*
la (by itself) *you, her, it*
la carne *the meat*
bistecca *steak*
insalata *salad*
prende *you take, he, she, it takes*

Bruno E Lei Signora Palmer?

Edith Prendo del pollo e un bicchiere d'acqua, per favore.

(Più tardi)

Bruno Prendiamo della frutta, o forse meglio – il tiramisù? No? Niente? Abbiamo finito? Un caffè per qualcuno? Nessuno? Bene, il conto, per favore!

Edith Signor Verdi, mi aiuti per favore! Come si dice in italiano 'doggy bag'? Vorrei un po' di carne per il mio cane.

Kate Ma Edith, il cane è in Inghilterra!

desidera *you would like, he, she, it would like*
cotoletta alla milanese *veal cutlet 'alla milanese'*
le patatine *the chips*
verdura *vegetables*
olio *oil*
prendo *I take*
pollo *chicken*
il bicchiere *the glass*
acqua *water*
frutta *fruit*
meglio *better*
finito *finished*
nessuno *nobody*
mi aiuti, per favore *help me, please*
come si dice in Italiano? *how do you say... in Italian?*

TOTAL NEW WORDS: 68
...only 95 words to go!

Last easy extras

The days of the week: *i giorni della settimana*

lunedì *Monday*
martedì *Tuesday*
mercoledì *Wednesday*
giovedì *Thursday*
venerdì *Friday*
sabato *Saturday*
domenica *Sunday*

Good news grammar

1 The past: team players and rebels

Remember **comprare, mangiare** and **riparare**: they all end in **-are**? Let's call them team players, because when you use them in the past, to say that you *did* or *have done* something, they all end in **-ato**.

...Ho compr**ato**/ mangi**ato**/ripar**ato**.

Here are three more team players:

lavorare	→	lavor**ato**
aiutare	→	aiut**ato**
telefonare	→	telefon**ato**

Then there are a couple of players from a neighbouring team. They end in **-ere** and finish up with **-uto** in the past.

conoscere	(*to know*)	→	conosci**uto**	(*known*)
credere	(*to believe*)	→	cred**uto**	(*believed*)

Finally the rebels: relax, there are only five.

dire	(*to say*)	→	**detto**	(*said*)
prendere	(*to take*)	→	**preso**	(*taken*)
fare	(*to do*)	→	**fatto**	(*done*)
vedere	(*to see*)	→	**visto**	(*seen*)
scrivere	(*to write*)	→	**scritto**	(*written*)

Spend 10 minutes practising the mental acrobatics. It's quite simple once you use them.

Chi lo ha **detto?** Cosa ha **preso?** Cosa ha **fatto?**
Ha **visto** Luigi? Ho **scritto** a Maria.

Remember, if you ever 'lose' a verb or verb form, you'll find it in the verb summary, page 70.

2 'It' and 'them'

Imagine you are talking about things – *wine, the company, holidays* or *seats on the plane*. Now imagine you are referring to these things. You would say *it* or *them*.

In Italian *it* is **lo** or **la**, and *them* is **li** or **le**, depending whether the things you are referring to are masculine or feminine, or one thing or more.

Compro **vino**	lo compro	*I buy it*
Compra **la ditta**	la compra	*You/he/she/buys it*
Ha le **vacanze** in aprile	le ha in aprile	*he has them*
Abbiamo **posti**	li abbiamo	*we have them*

Did you notice?... The *it* or *them* always goes in front of the verb.

***It** I buy*, ***It** you buy?*, ***Them** we have.*

3 Last quick verb box – *dovere*: must, have to

Three minutes should do it, now you know the pattern.

devo – deve – dobbiamo – devono

Learn by heart

Here is a short piece about someone who is rather fed up. Put yourself in his shoes ... Learn it and act it out in under 50 seconds.

Non mi piace ...

A Conosce il Signor Martini?
Ha telefonato ieri. Devo andare a mangiare con lui.

B Perché?

A È un buon cliente della ditta.
Però non è simpatico – mangia e beve troppo.

B E quando?

A Stasera! C'è il calcio in televisione.
Vorrei dire che sono malato ... ma non posso...
Sempre la ditta...!

B Ah ... mi dispiace!

Say it simply

When people want to speak Italian but don't dare it's usually because they are trying to *translate* what they want to say from English into Italian. But because they don't know some of the words they give up!

With **Instant Italian** you work around the words you don't know with the words you do know! And believe me, 380 words are enough to say anything!

It may not always be very elegant, but who cares? You are speaking, *communicating!*

Here are three examples, showing you how to say things in a simple way. The English words which are not part of the **Instant** vocabulary have been highlighted.

1 You need to **change your flight** to London from Tuesday to Friday.

This is what you could say – simply:

Non possiamo andare martedì, vorremmo andare venerdì.
or:
Martedì non va bene per noi. Venerdì è meglio.

2 You want to get your **purse** and **mobile phone** from the coach which the driver has locked.

Say it simply:

Mi dispiace. I miei soldi e il mio piccolo telefono sono sul'autobus.
or:
Ho bisogno di qualcosa importante. Mi dispiace molto, ma tutto è sul'autobus.

3 This time your friend has **just broken** the **heel** of her only pair of shoes. You have to catch a train and **need some help now.**
This is what you could say:

Scusi, la scarpa è rotta, e abbiamo poco tempo. C'è un negozio qui dove riparano le scarpe al momento?

Let's speak Italian

Here are eight sentences to say in Italian, and then on to greater things!

1 I am sorry, I do not have time.
2 Are we going with him?
3 I would like a salad.
4 We have been here yesterday.
5 Excuse me, what did you say?
6 I did not take this.
7 When did you work in Italy?
8 We did not do anything.

Now pretend you are in Italy with English friends who do not speak Italian. They will want you to ask people things and will want *you* to do it for them in Italian. They will say: 'Please ask him...' Start with **Scusi...**

9 ...if he has seen Mr Rossi.
10 ...where he bought the stamps.
11 ...if he has an appointment now.
12 ...where the restaurant is.

Now your friends will ask you to *tell* people things. They use some words which you don't know, so you have to use your **Instant** words. They will say: 'Please tell her that...' Start your sentence with **Mi dispiace,...**

13 ...her pasta is cold.
14 ...we are not having wine, only water.
15 ...she is a vegetarian.
16 ...he does not have his number.

While shopping you are offered various items. You take them all, saying 'yes, I take it' or 'yes, I take them'.

17 ...e la frutta?
18 ...e i gelati?
19 ...e le birre?
20 ...e il Signor Walker?

Answers

1 Mi dispiace, non ho tempo.
2 Andiamo con lui?
3 Vorrei un' insalata.
4 Siamo stati (*or* state) qui ieri.
5 Scusi, cosa ha detto?
6 Non ho preso questo.
7 Quando ha lavorato in Italia?
8 Non abbiamo fatto niente.
9 Scusi, ha visto il Signor Rossi?
10 Scusi, dove ha comprato i francobolli?
11 Scusi, ha un appuntamento adesso?
12 Scusi, dov'è il ristorante?
13 Mi dispiace, ma la sua pasta è fredda.
14 Mi dispiace, ma non abbiamo vino, solo acqua.
15 Mi dispiace, ma non mangia carne.
16 Mi dispiace, ma non ha il suo numero.
17 Sì, la prendo.
18 Sì, li prendo.
19 Sì, le prendo.
20 Sì, lo prendo.

Spot the keys

You practised listening for key words when you asked the way to the post office in Week 3. Now you are in a department store. You have asked the sales assistant if the black dress you liked is also available in size 44 (Italian).

She said **no** then **un momento, per favore** and disappeared. When she came back this is what she said:

> *Ho appena guardato in magazzino se ne rimaneva* **una nella sua taglia, ma c'è solo in verde. Ma questo** *modello è tagliato piuttosto* **grande**, *quindi* **credo che la taglia quarantadue** *possa* **andare bene per Lei**.

It appears that size 44 was only available in green but she felt that size 42 might be big enough.

Test your progress

1 Did you say that somebody has telephoned? Signor Gucci?
2 I would like to know where the restaurants are.
3 It is late and he is not there. What are we doing tonight?
4 Here is the menu! Do you know the wines of (the) Tuscany?
5 The cash dispenser is upstairs, behind the exit, near the door.
6 Wednesday we must go to the doctor. It is an important appointment.
7 Why do you say she is boring? Because I know her well.
8 Have you seen him? I must go to Pisa with him.
9 (The) Signor Rossini is my client. He has bought everything.
10 I would like to buy this thing. How does one say in Italian...?
11 Next week? I am sorry. It is not possible.
12 There is too much. Please help me. Many thanks!
13 One hundred thousand lire for two days. Very interesting. Yes, of course we take it.
14 I must buy three things for my friends.
15 He says that he has a cold and that he has not finished his work.
16 Can they eat only the minestrone?
17 Please help me. There is a terrible dog.
18 Nobody has seen who has eaten the steak.
19 Can I say something: the chicken is not bad, but the fish is better.
20 What do you take? The fruit? Yes, sure, it is from (the) Tuscany.

How are your 'shares' looking on the **Progress chart**? Going up?

05 week five

How about 15 minutes on the train, tube or bus, 10 minutes on the way home and 20 minutes before switching on the television...?

Day one

- Read **On the move.**
- Listen to/Read **In viaggio.**
- Read the **New words.** Learn 15 or more.

Day two

- Repeat **In viaggio** and the **New words.**
- Cut out the **Flash words** and get stuck in.

Day three

- Test yourself to perfection on all the **New words.**
- Listen to/Read **Learn by heart.**

Day four

- Read and learn the **Good news grammar.**
- Cut out and learn the **Flash sentences.**

Day five

- Listen to/Read **Let's speak Italian.**
- Listen to/Read **Spot the keys.**

Day six

- Translate **Test your progress.**

Day seven

How is the Progress chart looking? Great?... Great!
I bet you don't want a day off ... but I insist!

On the move

Tom and Kate are travelling through the lakes of Northern Italy – by train, bus and hire car. They talk to Nina, the ticket clerk at the station, to Jim on the train and later to Mario, the bus driver.

At the station

Tom Two tickets for Como, please.

Nina Thereandback?

Tom There and what? Can you speak more slowly please.

Nina There – and – back?

Tom No, one way only. At what time is there a train and from which platform?

Nina At 9.56. Platform eight.

Kate Quickly Tom, here are two seats, non-smoking. Oh, but someone is smoking. Excuse me, you (one) cannot smoke, because it is non-smoking here. It is forbidden to smoke.

Jim I am sorry. I don't understand. I speak only English.

At the bus stop

Kate There is no bus. We have to wait 20 minutes. Tom, here are my postcards. Over there is a letterbox. I would like to take some photos. The lake is beautiful with the sun.

Tom Kate, quickly! There are a lot of people. Here are two buses! Both are blue. This one is full. Let's take the other one. *(On the bus)* Two for Milan, please.

Mario This bus goes only to Como.

Tom But we are in Como!

Mario Yes, yes, but this is the bus for the hospital of Como.

In the car

Tom Here is our car. Only 150,000 lire for three days. I am very pleased.

Kate I do not like the car. It costs so little because it is very old. Let's hope that we don't have problems.

Tom I am sorry. The first car was too expensive and the second (one) too big. This was the last one.

(Later) Where are we? The map has disappeared! On the left there is a petrol station, and on the right there is a school. Come on, quickly!

→ Page 58

In viaggio

Tom and Kate are travelling through the lakes of Northern Italy – by train, bus and hire car. They talk to Nina, the ticket clerk at the station, to Jim on the train and later to Mario, the bus driver.

Alla stazione

Tom Due biglietti per Como per favore.

Nina Andataeritorno?

Tom Andata e cosa? Può parlare più lentamente per favore.

Nina Andata – e – ritorno?

Tom No, solo andata. A che ora c'è un treno e da che binario?

Nina Alle nove e cinquantasei. Binario otto.

Kate Presto Tom, qui ci sono due posti 'non fumatori'. Oh, ma qualcuno fuma. Scusi, non si può fumare, perché qui è 'non fumatori'. È proibito fumare.

Jim I am sorry. Non capisco. Parlo only English.

Alla fermata dell'autobus

Kate Non c'è l'autobus. Dobbiamo aspettare venti minuti. Tom, ecco le mie cartoline. Là c'è una buca delle lettere. Vorrei fare delle foto. Il lago è bellissimo con il sole!

Tom Kate, presto! C'è molta gente. Ecco due autobus! Tutti e due sono blu. Questo è pieno. Prendiamo l'altro.
(Nel autobus) Due per Milano per favore.

Mario Quest'autobus va solo fino a Como.

Tom Ma siamo a Como!

Mario Sì, sì, ma questo è l'autobus per l'ospedale di Como.

In auto

Tom Ecco la nostra auto. Solo 150.000 lire per tre giorni. Sono molto contento.

Kate L'auto non mi piace. Costa così poco perché è molto vecchia. Speriamo di non avere problemi.

Tom Mi dispiace. La prima auto era troppo cara e la seconda troppo grande. Questa era l'ultima.
(Più tardi) Dove siamo? La cartina è sparita! A sinistra c'è un benzinaio e a destra c'è una scuola. Dai, presto!

→ Page 59

Kate We are coming from the underground station. The main road is at the traffic light. It's perhaps three kilometres to the motorway. *(On the motorway)* Why does the car go so slowly? Have we enough petrol? How many litres? Do we have oil? Is the engine not too hot? They have given us a broken car. Where is the mobile phone? Where is the number of the mechanic (garage)? Where is my bag?

Tom Kate, **please**! All this gives me a headache. And now comes also the rain! And why are the police behind us?

New words

in viaggio *on the move, travelling*
la stazione (railway) *station*
biglietto *ticket*
andata e ritorno *return ticket* ('gone and return')
parlare *(to) speak*
più *more*
lentamente *slowly*
treno *train*
binario *track, platform*
presto *quick, quickly*
non fumatori *non-smoking*
fuma *he/she/it smokes, you smoke*
fumare *(to) smoke*
proibito *forbidden*
non capisco *I don't understand*
parlo *I speak*
fermata *stop*
aspettare *(to) wait*
cartolina *postcard*
buca delle lettere *letter box*
la foto, le foto *the photo, the photos*
lago *lake*
bellissimo/a *very beautiful*
il sole *the sun*
la gente *the people*
tutti e due *both* ('all and two')
pieno/a *full*
altro/a *other*
l'ospedale *the hospital*
l'auto (la) *the car*
giorno, giorni *day, days*
contento/a *pleased, happy*
mi piace/non mi piace *I like/ I do not like*
così *so*
vecchio/a *old*
speriamo *we hope, let's hope*
i problemi *the problems*
primo/a *first*
secondo/a *second*
ultimo/a *last*
cartina *map*
sparito/a *disappeared*
benzinaio *petrol station*
dai! *come on!*
veniamo *we come, we are coming*
strada principale *main road*
semaforo *traffic light*
chilometro *kilometre*
autostrada *motorway*
benzina *petrol*
litro, litri *litre, litres*

Kate Veniamo dalla fermata del metro. La strada principale è al semaforo. Sono forse tre chilometri fino all'autostrada. *(In autostrada)* Perché l'auto va così lentamente? Abbiamo abbastanza benzina? Quanti litri? Abbiamo olio? Il motore non è troppo caldo? Ci hanno dato un auto rotta. Dov'è il telefonino? Dov'è il numero del meccanico? Dov'è la mia borsa?

Tom Kate, **per favore!** Tutto questo mi fa venire il mal di testa! E adesso viene anche la pioggia! E perché c'è la polizia dietro di noi?

il motore *the motor, engine*
caldo/a *hot*
ci *us*
dare/dato *give/given*
telefonino *mobile phone*
meccanico *mechanic (at a garage)*
fa *he/she/it makes, you make*
venire *(to) come*
il mal di testa *the headache*
pioggia *rain*
polizia *police*
noi *us, we*

TOTAL NEW WORDS: 63
...only 32 words to go!

Learn by heart

Someone has pranged the car and someone else is getting suspicious...! Try to say these lines fluently and like a prize-winning play!

Andiamo al tennis

A Andiamo al tennis. Mi piacciono i due Americani.
Ho dei biglietti della mia ditta.
Prendiamo l'autobus, o meglio, il metro.
C'è anche un treno tutto il giorno.

B L'autobus? Il metro? Un treno?
Perché? Cosa c'è? Abbiamo un auto laggiù*.

A Beh... ieri, colla pioggia, non ho visto il semaforo.
Però è poco, solo la porta, e il meccanico era molto simpatico!

***laggiù:** *down there*

Good news grammar

1 Confusing: *mi, me, Lei, gli, ci, noi, la, lo, lui, lei*

You have come across these little words in the stories and the **New words**. Some appeared before the verbs ...**ci hanno dato**: *they have given us*, and some were stuck onto the end...**Posso aiutarla**? Can I help you? or **Può farlo**: *Can you do it?* Feel like pulling out your hair?

Learning these little words 'cold' is quite difficult, but when they come up in the **Flash sentences** or the texts it's not so bad. And when you speak **Instant Italian** you can muddle them up or avoid them altogether. No problem.

I have extracted six easy and useful ones. Spend five minutes learning them and take another five minutes to remember them.

for me	per **me**	*for her*	per **lei**
for you	per **Lei**	*for us*	per **noi**
for him	per **lui**	*for them*	per **loro**

You use the same words with **con, a** and **da.**

con me: *with me*, **a Lei:** *to you*, **da loro:** *from them*, or *at their house*.

2 *Mi piace – non mi piace*

You will use this all the time. Think how often you use *I like – I don't like* in English!

You can like or not like *things* or *doing things*:

Mi piace la sua scuola. **Mi piace** mangiare con lui. **Non mi piace** il pesce. **Mi piace** molto!

If you like more than one thing, you say **mi piacciono: mi piacciono** i negozi; **non mi piacciono** i ristoranti.

3 A reminder: *ho bisogno*

Remember **ho bisogno** from Week 1?

Ho bisogno di molti soldi. It literally means *I have need of* … .
This is just a reminder to use it.
Ho bisogno di un medico.
Abbiamo bisogno di un meccanico … Anche noi!

Let's speak Italian

A ten-point warm-up: I give you an answer and you ask me a question as if you did not hear the words in CAPITAL LETTERS very well.

Example Lucìa è ALLA POSTA.
Ask Dov'è Lucìa?

1 Il telefonino è NELLA MIA BORZA.
2 Sono stato in ospedale IN MARZO.
3 Tom vorrebbe parlare CON MARCELLO.
4 Per Pisa, andata e ritorno costa 86.000 LIRE.
5 Non abbiamo visto IL SEMAFORO.
6 Sì, sono contento della scuola.
7 NO, la cartina non mi piace.
8 Vanno in Inghilterra CON LA FERRARI.
9 La casa non mi piace PERCHÉ È MOLTO VECCHIA.
10 Le vacanze erano BELLISIME.

Answer in Italian using 'yes' or 'no'. Speak about yourself.

11 Ha visto il benzinaio?
12 Prende questo treno?
13 Va adesso alla stazione?
14 Le piace il lago?
15 Può fumare qui?

Explain these words in Italian. Your answers can differ from mine.

16 daily help
17 kennel
18 teacher
19 unemployed
20 to be broke

Answers

1 Dov'è il telefonino?
2 Quando è stato in ospedale?
3 Con chi vorrebbe parlare Tom?
4 Quanto costa per Pisa, andata e ritorno?
5 Cosa non ha visto?
6 È contento della scuola?
7 Le piace la cartina?
8 Come vanno in Inghilterra?
9 Perché non le piace la casa?
10 Com' erano le vacanze?
11 Sì, l'ho visto/No, non l'ho visto.
12 Sì, lo prendo. No, non lo prendo.
13 Sì, vado adesso. No, non vado adesso.
14 Sì, mi piace. No, non mi piace.
15 Sì, qui posso fumare. No, qui non posso fumare.
16 Una signora che aiuta in casa con tutto il lavoro.
17 Una casa per il cane quando siamo in vacanza.
18 Qualcuno che lavora nella scuola con i bambini.
19 Qualcuno che non ha lavoro.
20 Non abbiamo più soldi. Sono finiti.

Spot the keys

This time you plan a trip in the country and wonder about the weather.

You **Scusi, vorrei sapere che tempo fa.**

Answer **Non so cosa** *dicano le previsioni* **in televisione** *ma mi sembra di avere capito che c'è una perturbazione che arriva. Farà ancora piuttosto* **caldo, più o meno venticinque** *gradi, ma prima di* **stasera** *avremo sicuramente della* **pioggia**.

He doesn't know something on television (?) but you heard the word **hot** and then **more or less 25** (degrees centigrade). You also understood **this evening** and **rain**. Perhaps you'd better take an umbrella!

Test your progress

1 It is forbidden to go to the restaurant without shoes.
2 I like your Lamborghini. Was it very cheap?
3 When I am travelling (on the move) I always speak a lot of Italian.
4 I need six tickets. Are there non-smoking seats?
5 Let's hope we don't have (not to have) problems with the engine.
6 I do not like the Internet. It is difficult. I believe I am (to be) too old.
7 I do not understand. Can you speak more slowly, please?
8 It is hot and there are a lot of people here. Let's go to the lake.
9 One hour with her gives me (me makes come) a headache.
10 There is a bus at the traffic lights. Where is it going?
11 The credit card has (is) gone. We have to telephone the police.
12 Let's do it like this: first we buy the Ferrari for me and afterwards a T-shirt for you.
13 I like this car, but the other (one) was better.
14 We have only a litre of petrol and there is not a petrol station until Naples.
15 I like the sun and I like the rain. I like both.
16 *(On the phone)* Hello, we are 20 km from Pisa. Is there a mechanic?
17 Excuse me, can you help me, please? I do not know Rome. Where is the station?
18 The main street? It is not difficult if you take the metro.
19 Where are they? What have they done? I do not like to wait.
20 We are coming from (the) platform 17? Where is Mario?

06 week six

This is your last week! Need I say more?

Day one

- Read **In the airport.**
- Listen to/Read **In aeroporto.**
- Read the **New words.** There are only 32!

Day two

- Repeat **In aeroporto** and learn all the **New words.**
- Work with the **Flash words** and **Flash sentences.**

Day three

- Test yourself on the **Flash sentences.**
- No more **Good news grammar!** Have a look at the summary.

Day four

- Listen to/Read and learn **Arrivederci!**
- Read **Say it simply.**

Day five

- Listen to/Read **Spot the keys.**
- Listen to/Read **Let's speak Italian.**

Day six

- Your last **Test your progress!** Go for it!

Day seven

Congratulations!

You have successfully completed the course and can now speak

Instant Italian!

In the airport

Tom and Kate are on their way home to Birmingham. They are in the departure lounge of Milan airport.

Tom On Monday we must work. Terrible! I would rather go to Miami or Honolulu. Nobody knows where I am and the office can wait.

Kate And **my** company? What do they do? They speak with my mother! She has the number of our mobile. And then?

Tom Yes, yes, I know (it). Well, perhaps at Christmas we'll go for a week on the snow or to Madeira on a ship... There is a kiosk down there. I'll go and buy a newspaper. ...Kate! There is Gino Pavarotti!

Gino Hello, how are you? What are you doing here? This is my wife, Nancy. Are the holidays over? How were they?

Kate Italy is wonderful. We have seen a lot and eaten too much. Now we know Tuscany and the lakes very well.

Gino Next year Venice! What a fantastic city!... Mrs Walker, my wife would like to buy a book about computers. Can you go with her and help her, please? Mr Walker, you have the newspaper. Are there any photos of the football? And then are we going to drink something?

(At the kiosk)

Kate There is nothing here. I do not see anything of interest. Are you also going to England?

Nancy No, we are going to Pisa to Gino's mother. Our children are often with her during the holidays. Tomorrow we'll take the train. It costs less.

Kate Your husband works at the Bank of Italy?

Nancy Yes. The work is interesting, but the money is little. We have an apartment (which is) too small for us and an old car. It always needs a lot of repairs. My family lives in California and my girlfriend is in Florida and we write a lot of letters. I would like to go to America but it is too expensive.

Kate But you have a beautiful house in Portofino.

Nancy A house in Portofino? I have never been to Portofino. When we have holidays we go to a friend in Genoa.

→ Page 68

In aeroporto

Tom and Kate are on their way home to Birmingham. They are in the departure lounge of Milano airport.

Tom Lunedì dobbiamo lavorare. Terribile! Vorrei invece andare a Miami o a Honolulu. Nessuno sa dove sono e la ditta può aspettare.

Kate E la **mia** ditta? Cosa fanno? Parlano con mia madre! Lei ha il numero del nostro telefonino. E poi...?

Tom Sì, sì, lo so. Allora forse a Natale andiamo una settimana sulla neve o a Madeira in nave. ...C'è un chiosco laggiù. Vado a comprare un giornale...Kate! C'è Gino Pavarotti!

Gino Salve! Come va? Cosa fa qui? Questa è mia moglie Nancy. Sono finite le vacanze? Come sono state?

Kate L'Italia è meravigliosa! Abbiamo visto molto e mangiato troppo. Adesso conosciamo la Toscana e i laghi molto bene.

Gino Il prossimo anno Venezia! Che città fantastica!... Signora Walker, mia moglie vorrebbe comprare un libro di computer. Per favore, può andare con lei e aiutarla? Signor Walker, Lei ha il giornale. Ci sono delle foto del calcio? E poi andiamo a bere qualcosa?

(Al chiosco)

Kate Qui non c'è niente. Non vedo niente di interessante. Va anche Lei in Inghilterra?

Nancy No, andiamo a Pisa dalla madre di Gino. I nostri bambini sono spesso da lei durante le vacanze. Domani prendiamo il treno. Costa meno.

Kate Suo marito lavora alla Banca d'Italia?

Nancy Sì. Il lavoro è interessante, ma i soldi sono pochi. Abbiamo un appartamento troppo piccolo per noi e una vecchia auto. Ha bisogno sempre di molte riparazioni. La mia famiglia vive in California e la mia amica è in Florida e ci scriviamo molte lettere. Vorrei andare in America ma costa troppo.

Kate Ma Lei ha una bella casa a Portofino.

Nancy Una casa a Portofino? Non sono mai stata a Portofino. Quando abbiamo le vacanze andiamo a Genova da un amico.

→ Page 69

Tom Kate, come on, quickly. We must go. Goodbye! What is the matter, Kate? What did Mrs Pavarotti say?

Kate Wait, Tom, wait...!

New words

aeroporto *airport*
invece *instead, on the other hand*
la madre *the mother*
sa *he/she/it knows, you know*
fanno *they do, make*
parlano *they speak*
lo so *I know (it)*
Natale *Christmas*
la neve *the snow*
la nave *the ship*
chiosco *kiosk*
laggiù *down there*
salve *hello* (not quite as familiar as *ciao)*
come va? *how are you?*
meraviglioso/a *wonderful*
conosciamo *we know*
città *town, city*
fantastico/a *fantastic*
vorrebbe *he/she/it would like, you would like*
libro *book*
vedo *I see*
durante *during*
spesso *often*
appartamento *apartment, flat*
le riparazioni *the repairs*
famiglia *family*
vive *he/she/it lives, you live*
scriviamo *we write*
lettera/lettere *letter, letters*
mai *never, ever*
che cosa c'è? *what's the matter?*
aspetta/aspetti! *wait!* (familiar), *wait!* (polite)

TOTAL NEW WORDS: 32
TOTAL ITALIAN WORDS LEARNED: 379
EXTRA WORDS: 74

GRAND TOTAL: 453

Tom Kate, dai, presto. Dobbiamo andare. Arrivederci! Che cosa c'è, Kate? Cosa ha detto la Signora Pavarotti?

Kate Aspetta,Tom, aspetta...!

Learn by heart

This is your last dialogue to learn by heart. Give it your best! You now have six prize-winning party pieces, and a large store of everyday sayings which will be very useful.

Arrivederci...!

Kate Pronto. Buongiorno Signor Verdi. Sono Kate Walker.
Siamo all'aeroporto. Sì, le vacanze sono finite.
Che bella, l'Italia!
Tom vorrebbe parlare con Lei. Un momento per favore e... arrivederci!

Tom Ciao, Bruno! Cosa? Ha comprato tutti e due?
C'è un e-mail nella ditta?
Benissimo! Mille grazie!
L'anno prossimo? Kate vorrebbe andare a Capri,
ma io vorrei vedere* Venezia.
Con Edith Palmer? **Per favore**!
Dobbiamo andare. Dunque... a presto! Ciao! Arrivederci!

***vedere**: *(to) see*

Good news grammar

As promised there is no new grammar in this lesson, just a summary of all the **Instant** verbs which appear in the six weeks. The 31 verbs are not for learning, just for a quick check. You know and have used most of them!

Basic form	**I**	**you, he, she, it**	**we**	**they**	**Past**
avere	ho	ha	abbiamo	hanno	avuto
aiutare	aiuto	aiuta	aiutiamo	aiutano	aiutato
andare	vado	va	andiamo	vanno	(sono) andato
aspettare	aspetto	aspetta	aspettiamo	aspettano	aspettato
bere	bevo	beve	beviamo	bevono	bevuto
capire	capisco	capisce	capiamo	capiscono	capito
comprare	compro	compra	compriamo	comprano	comprato
conoscere	conosco	conosce	conosciamo	conoscono	conosciuto
costare		costa		costano	
credere	credo	crede	crediamo	credono	creduto
dare	do	da	diamo	danno	dato
desiderare	desidero	desidera	desideramo	desiderano	desiderato
dire	dico	dice	diciamo	dicono	detto
dovere	devo	deve	dobbiamo	devono	dovuto
essere	sono	è	siamo	sono	(sono) stato
(*imperf.*)	era	era	eramo	erano	
fare	faccio	fa	facciamo	fanno	fatto
fumare	fumo	fuma	fumiamo	fumano	fumato
lavorare	lavoro	lavora	lavoriamo	lavorano	lavorato
mangiare	mangio	mangia	mangiamo	mangiano	mangiato
parlare	parlo	parla	parliamo	parlano	parlato
passare	passo	passa	passiamo	passono	passato
potere	posso	può	possiamo	possono	potuto
prendere	prendo	prende	prendiamo	prendono	preso
riparare	riparo	ripara	ripariamo	riparono	riparato
sapere	so	sa	sappiamo	sanno	saputo
scrivere	scrivo	scrive	scriviamo	scrivono	scritto
sperare	spero	spera	speriamo	sperano	sperato
telefonare	telefono	telefona	telefoniamo	telefonano	telefonato
vedere	vedo	vede	vediamo	vedono	visto
venire	vengo	viene	veniamo	vengono	sono venuto
(volere)	vorrei	vorrebbe	vorremmo	vorrebbero	

Say it simply

1 Imagine you are at the dry cleaner's. You want to know if the item you have brought to be cleaned can be done by the end of the day since you are leaving for Verona early tomorrow morning. You also want to explain that the stain may be red wine.

Think of what you could say in simple Italian, using the words you know. Then write it down and compare it with my suggestion on page 78.

2 You are at the airport, about to catch your flight home when you realize that you have left some clothes behind in the room of your hotel. You phone the hotel's housekeeper to ask her to send the things on to you.

What would you say? Formulate your telephone call and say it. Then write it down and compare it with the one on page 78.

Spot the keys

Here are two final practice rounds. If you have the recording, close the book now.

1 This time, the key words are not shown. When you have found them see if you can get the gist of it. My answer is on page 78.

This is what you might ask of a taxi driver:

A quanti minuti è l'aeroporto e quanto costa?

And this could be the reply:

Dipende da quando va. Normalemente ci vogliono venti minuti, ma se c'è traffico e se c'è la coda sul ponte ci metterà almeno trentacinque minuti. Il prezzo lo può vedere sul tachimetro. Più o meno saranno dalle trenta alle trentacinque mila lire.

2 While in the departure lounge of the airport, you overheard someone raving about something. Identify the key words and guess where they have been. The answer is on page 78.

... e anche mio marito dice che delle vacanze così gli piacciono moltissimo, molto di più di quelle dello scorso anno. La gente era proprio simpatica e molto più amabile che da noi. L'hotel era situato proprio in riva al lago; abbiamo fatto delle belle camminate e il tempo è stato bellissimo. Abbiamo mangiato benissimo e il prossimo anno ci ritorneremo certamente in...

Let's speak Italian

Here's a five-point warm-up: answer these questions using the words in brackets.

1 Ha comprato l'appartamento? (sì, lo)
2 Sa che fanno a Natale? (sì, niente)
3 Quando ha visto suo marito? (ieri)
4 Perchè va in Inghilterra? (famiglia, vive, là)
5 Com'è l'Italia? (meravigliosa)

In your last exercise you are going to interpret again, this time telling your Italian friend what others have said in English. Each time say the whole sentence OUT LOUD, translating the English words in brackets.

6 Il mio amico ha detto che... (*the holidays are finished*).
7 Ha detto anche che... (*we are going to Venice next year*).
8 Mia moglie vorrebbe sapere... (*when you go to Los Angeles*).
9 Vorrebbe anche sapere... (*what they said*).
10 Mio marito dice che... (*he cannot come*).
11 Angela non può venire perché... (*she works on a ship*).
12 Il mio amico dice che... (*you are very nice*).
13 Dice anche che... (*he would like to have your phone number*).
14 C'è qualcuno che vorrebbe sapere... (*what you did*).
15 Mia madre dice che... (*she likes the shops*).
16 Nessuno sa... (*where he has been in America*).
17 I miei amici non sanno... (*who took the car*).
18 Qualcuno sa... (*how one can go to Lago Maggiore*).
19 Non so... (*how much the repairs cost*).
20 Kate Walker sa... (*where you can buy* **Instant Italian**).

Answers

1 Sì, l'ho comprato.
2 Sì, non fanno niente.
3 L'ho visto ieri.
4 Perché la mia famiglia vive là.
5 L'Italia è meravigliosa.
6 ...le nostre vacanze sono finite.
7 ...andiamo a Venezia l'anno prossimo.
8 ...quando va a Los Angeles.
9 ...cosa hanno detto.
10 ...non può venire.
11 ...lavora su una nave.
12 ...Lei è molto simpatico/a.
13 ...vorrebbe avere il suo numero di telefono.
14 ...cosa ha fatto.
15 ...le piacciono i negozi.
16 ...dov'è stato in America.
17 ...chi ha preso l'auto.
18 ...come si può andare al Lago Maggiore.
19 ...quanto costano le riparazioni.
20 ...dove si può comprare **Instant Italian**.

Test your progress

Thirty **Instant** verbs have been crammed into this text! But don't panic – it looks worse than it is. Go for it – you'll do brilliantly!

Translate into Italian:

1. We write many letters because we have a new computer.
2. Hello, can I help? Your bag has gone? Where can it be?
3. Who knows the number of his mobile phone? I am sorry, I don't know it.
4. How are you? I am pleased that you do not smoke (any) more.
5. Would you like to see Bologna? It is a big town.
6. I do not like January. There is snow and it is often very cold.
7. There is a kiosk down there. Would you like something to drink?
8. Why have they not phoned? We waited until yesterday.
9. I'll take the book. He says that it is interesting.
10. I believe that the airport is always open, day and night.
11. It is important to know how much the client has bought.
12. Have you seen the English newspaper? I do not like the photo. It is ugly.
13. He said that he has (the) cold. He hopes to come tomorrow.
14. Is an apartment near the centre expensive in Italy?
15. We both have to work. Three boys and two girls cost a lot.
16. I am going at Christmas. I have (the) holidays in December instead of July.
17. We know Marcello very well. Do you like him?
18. Can you give me the dog? He is small but nice. What does he eat?
19. Her mother is here. She does not speak Italian. It is a little difficult for them.
20. Don't you know it? The repairs costs 500,000 lire.
21. I must go to the cash dispenser. I need money.
22. I am sorry but **Instant Italian** is now finished.

Check your answers on page 77. Now go to the **Progress chart** and work out your final score for the course. You'll be proud of yourself!

How to score

From a total of 100%

- Subtract 1% for each wrong or missing word.
- Subtract 1% for the wrong form of the verb. Example *we have* **ho (abbiamo).**
- Subtract 1% every time you mixed up the present and the past tenses.

There are no penalties for:

- wrong use of all those little words, like: **il, la, un, una, il suo, la sua, da il (dal), in il (nel),** etc.
- wrong ending of adjectives, e.g.e: **una amica americano.**
- wrong choice of words with similar meaning, e.g.: **a, in, da.**
- wrong or different word order
- wrong spelling/missing accents/missing apostrophes – as long as you can *say* the word, e.g.: **bisonyo (bisogno), com'e, comè (com'è).**

100% LESS YOUR PENALTIES WILL GIVE YOU YOUR WEEKLY SCORE

Week 1: Test your progress

1. Buongiorno, siamo Helen e Jane.
2. Sono di Roma, anche Lei?
3. Dove lavora adesso?
4. Sono stato/stata a Milano in ottobre.
5. La mia amica è in Italia per un anno.
6. Andiamo sempre a Pisa in giugno.
7. Ho lavorato alla Fiat in maggio.
8. Che cosa/cosa fa a Londra?
9. Lavoro in una scuola ma senza soldi.
10. La casa grande a Bologna è per i bambini.

11 Un momento, per favore, dov'è Luigi?
12 La casa ha il telefono? No purtroppo.
13 Costa molto la Ferrari? Sì, certo, costa troppo.
14 Com'è il lavoro in Italia? Buono?
15 Mario ha un amico/una amica in una ditta americana.
16 Siamo stati/state a Como per tre giorni.
17 Abbiamo i posti buoni in aereo.
18 Ho sempre le vacanze noiose.
19 Ho bisogno di una bella moglie, una Lamborghini e molti soldi...
20 Telefona adesso con una ditta a Londra.

	Correct your answers.
YOUR SCORE: ______ %	Then read them out loud twice.

Week 2: Test your progress

1 Dove c'è un telefono?
2 Scusi, abbiamo solo la carta di credito.
3 Possiamo mangiare alle sette domani?
4 Ha una tavola abbastanza grande? Siamo in cinque.
5 Le camere piccole non hanno il bagno.
6 Vorremmo mangiare prosciutto e melone.
7 Possiamo andare dalle sei alle sette meno un quarto.
8 Dove possiamo bere qualcosa?
9 Siamo stati al bar dalle nove alle dieci e mezza.
10 Va bene, prendiamo la Fiat per un giorno.
11 Quanto costa la prima colazione? Solo seimila lire.
12 Andiamo a riparare il computer. È rotto.
13 Com'è il latte? Il bambino lo può bere?
14 Dove sono i servizi, a destra o a sinistra?
15 Posso andare a Hollywood – senza mio marito?
16 Un caffè per favore – niente per Lei?
17 Dov'è la Signora Rossi? Forse nel bar?
18 Cinquemila lire per un tè freddo – è un po'caro...!
19 Sono stato in Toscana in febbraio. Non è male.
20 Ci sono trecento bar qui, uno a cento metri da qui.

YOUR SCORE: ___ %

Week 3: Test your progress

1 Prima vorrei passare dal Bankomat.
2 In questo negozio le scarpe constano troppo.
3 Ha visto mio marito in farmacia?
4 Siamo stati qui fino alle dieci e un quarto.

5 Abbiamo visto il tennis in Inghilterra, in televisione.
6 Mi dispiace, non abbiamo lo stesso in rosso, nella taglia 44.
7 Questo negozio non è conveniente.
8 Chi ha riparato il mio telefono? Lei?
9 Ecco il grande magazzino. Però non è aperto!
10 Oggi non abbiamo comprato troppo, solo pane e mezzo chilo di burro.
11 Ho mangiato tutto – uova, mele, patate e un pezzo di formaggio.
12 Dobbiamo fare spese. È questo il centro?
13 Ieri sono stato/stata in ditta fino alle nove.
14 I giornali inglesi costano molto in Italia.
15 C'è un autobus? No? Non importa.
16 Era un commesso molto simpatico.
17 Cos'è questo? Qualcosa per noi?
18 Ha comprato la borsa qui vicino o alla' UPIM?
19 Era tutto molto caro. Dunque non ho comprato niente.
20 Abbiamo bisogno di tre chili, credo.

YOUR SCORE: ___ %

Week 4: Test your progress

1 Ha detto che qualcuno ha telefonato? Il Signor Gucci?
2 Vorrei sapere dove sono i ristoranti.
3 È tardi e non c'è. Cosa facciamo stasera?
4 Ecco il menù! Conosce i vini della Toscana?
5 Il Bankomat è su, dietro all'uscita, vicino alla porta.
6 Mercoledì dobbiamo andare dal medico. È un appuntamento importante.
7 Perché dice che è noiosa? Perché la conosco bene.
8 Lo ha visto? Devo andare a Pisa con lui.
9 Il Signor Rossini è il mio cliente. Ha comprato tutto.
10 Vorrei comprare questa cosa. Come si dice in italiano…?
11 La settimana prossima? Mi dispiace. Non è possibile.
12 C'è troppo. Mi aiuti per favore. Grazie mille!
13 Centomila lire per due giorni? Molto interessante. Sì, naturalmente lo/la prendiamo.
14 Devo comprare tre cose per i miei amici.
15 Dice che ha il raffreddore e che non ha finito il suo lavoro.
16 Possono mangiare solo il minestrone?
17 Mi aiuti per favore. C'è un cane terribile.
18 Nessuno ha visto chi ha mangiato la bistecca.
19 Posso dire qualcosa: il pollo non è male ma il pesce è meglio.
20 Cosa prende? La frutta? Sì certo, è dalla Toscana.

YOUR SCORE: ___ %

Week 5: Test your progress

1 È proibito andare al ristorante senza scarpe.
2 Mi piace la sua Lamborghini. Era molto conveniente?
3 Quando sono in viaggio parlo sempre molto italiano.
4 Ho bisogno di sei biglietti. Ci sono posti non fumatori?
5 Speriamo di non avere problemi con il motore.
6 Non mi piace l'Internet. È difficile. Credo di essere troppo vecchio/a.
7 Non capisco. Può parlare più lentamente per favore?
8 Fa caldo e c'è molta gente qui. Andiamo al lago!
9 Un'ora con lei mi fa venire il mal di testa.
10 C'è un autobus al semaforo. Dove va?
11 La carta di credito è sparita. Dobbiamo telefonare alla polizia.
12 Facciamo così: prima compriamo la Ferrari per me e dopo una T-shirt per Lei.
13 Mi piace quest' auto, pero l'altra era meglio.
14 Abbiamo solo un litro di benzina e non c'è un benzinaio fino a Napoli!
15 Mi piace il sole e mi piace la pioggia. Tutti e due mi piacciono.
16 Pronto. Siamo a venti chilometri da Pisa. C'è un meccanico?
17 Scusi, può aiutarmi per favore? Non conosco Roma. Dov'è la stazione?
18 La strada principale? Non è difficile si prende il metro.
19 Dove sono? Cosa hanno fatto? Non mi piace aspettare.
20 Veniamo dal binario diciassette, Dov'è Mario?

YOUR SCORE: ___ %

Week 6: Test your progress

1 Scriviamo molte lettere perché abbiamo un computer nuovo.
2 Salve, posso aiutare? La sua borsa è sparita? Dove può essere?
3 Chi sa il numero del suo telefonino? Mi dispiace, non lo so.
4 Come va? Sono contento che non fuma più.
5 Vorrebbe vedere Bologna? È una città grande.
6 Non mi piace gennaio. C'è neve e spesso fa molto freddo.
7 C'è un chiosco laggiù. Desidera qualcosa da bere?
8 Perché non hanno telefonato? Abbiamo aspettato fino a ieri.
9 Prendo il libro. Dice che è interessante.
10 Credo che l'aeroporto è sempre aperto, giorno e notte.
11 È importante sapere quanto ha comprato il cliente.
12 Ha visto il giornale inglese? Non mi piace la foto. È brutta!
13 Ha detto che ha il raffreddore. Spera di venire domani.

14 Un appartamento vicino al centro è caro in Italia?
15 Dobbiamo lavorare tutti e due. Tre bambini e due bambine costano molto.
16 Vado a Natale. Ho le vacanze a dicembre invece che a luglio.
17 Conosciamo Marcello molto bene. Le piace?
18 Può darmi il cane? È piccolo ma simpatico. Cosa mangia?
19 Sua madre è qui. Non parla italiano. È un po' difficile per loro.
20 Non lo sa? Le riparazioni costano cinquecentomila lire.
21 Devo passare dal Bankomat. Ho bisogno di soldi.
22 Mi dispiace, ma **Instant Italian** è finito adesso.

YOUR SCORE: ___ %

Week 6: Say it simply

1 ...Scusi, ho un grande problema. Forse è vino rosso ma non sono certa. Siamo all' hotel solo fino a domani. Andiamo a Verona alle sette. Lo può fare per stasera per favore?

2 Pronto. Buongiorno, sono Kate Walker. Telefono dall'aeroporto. Sono stata nella camera 22 per tre giorni. Mi dispiace ma ci sono delle mie cose nella camera e come ho detto siamo adesso all'aeroporto e andiamo a Birmingham. Può aiutarmi per favore? L'hotel sa dove sono (vivo) a Birmingham. Molte grazie.

Week 6: Spot the keys

1 It depends when you are going. Normally it takes 20 minutes. But if there is a lot of traffic and there is a queue on the bridge, it takes at least 35 minutes. You can read the price on the meter. It will be between 30,000 and 35,000 lire.

2 They had of course been in... *England!*

The **Flash cards** have been voted the best part of this course! Learning words and sentences can be tedious but with flash cards it's quick and good fun.

This is what you do

When the **Day-by-day guide** tells you to use the cards cut them out. There are 18 **Flash words** and 10 **Flash sentences** for each week. Each card has a little number on it telling you to which week it belongs. So you won't cut out too many cards at a time or muddle them up later on.

First try to learn the words and sentences by looking at both sides. Then, when you have a rough idea start testing yourself – that's the fun bit. Look at the English, say the Italian, and then check. Make a pile for the 'correct' ones and one for the 'wrong' and 'don't know' ones. When all cards are used up start again with the 'wrong' pile and try to whittle it down until you get all of them right. You can also play it 'backwards' by starting with the Italian face-up.

Keep the cards in a little box or put an elastic band around them. Take them with you on the bus, the train, to the hairdresser's or the dentist's.

If you find the paper too flimsy, photocopy the words and sentences onto card before cutting them up. You could also buy some plain card and stick them on or simply copy them out.

The 18 **Flash words** of each lesson are there to start you off. Convert the rest of the **New words** to **Flash cards**, too. It's well worth it!

Flash cards for Instant learning:
Don't lose them – use them!

1 abbiamo	1 siamo
1 purtroppo	1 andiamo
1 vado	1 sono stato/ sono stata
1 il mio, la mia	1 ditta
1 che, che cosa, cosa	1 fa
1 ho lavorato	1 adesso

1 we are	1 we have
1 we go, let's go	1 unfortunately
1 I was, I have been	1 I go
1 company, firm	1 my
1 you do, he/ she/it does	1 what
1 now	1 I worked, I have worked

1 siamo stati/e	1 come
1 com'è	1 ho bisogno(di)
1 sempre	1 senza
2 la camera	2 forse
2 abbastanza	2 un po'
2 male	2 quanto

1 how	1 we were, we have been
1 I need	1 how is?
1 without	1 always
2 perhaps	2 the room
2 a little	2 enough
2 how much	2 bad

2 va bene	2 la prima colazione
2 c'è	2 diritto
2 qualcosa	2 solo
2 il conto	2 troppo
2 poi	2 qui
2 a sinistra	2 a destra

2 breakfast	2 all right, OK
2 straight on	2 there is
2 only	2 something
2 too, too much	2 the bill
2 here	2 then
2 (on the) right	2 (on the) left

3 oggi	3 dobbiamo
3 tutto	3 dopo
3 fino a	3 quando
3 più tardi	3 pezzo
3 ieri	3 vicino
3 lo stesso	3 questo

3 we must	3 today
3 after, afterwards	3 all
3 when	3 until
3 piece	3 later
3 near	3 yesterday
3 this	3 the same

3 francobolli	3 comprare
3 credo	3 ho comprato
3 chi	3 aperto/a
4 qualcuno	4 perché?
4 un appuntamento	4 benissimo!
4 l'uscita	4 davanti a

[3] (to) buy	[3] stamps
[3] I have bought	[3] I believe
[3] open	[3] who
[4] why, *also*: because	[4] someone
[4] excellent!	[4] an appointment
[4] in front of	[4] the exit

4 stasera	4 che
4 dietro a	4 su
4 nessuno	4 meglio
4 certo	4 posso
4 come	4 una cosa
4 conosco	4 un bicchiere

4 that, *also*: what?	4 tonight
4 on	4 behind
4 better	4 nobody
4 I can	4 sure, certain
4 a thing, matter	4 like, as *also*: how?
4 a glass	4 I know

5 biglietto	5 aspettare
5 presto	5 fermata
5 altro/a	5 sparito/a
5 semaforo	5 caldo/a
5 pioggia	5 benzina
5 dare / dato	5 …mi piace

5 (to) wait	5 ticket
5 stop	5 quick, quickly
5 gone, disappeared	5 other
5 warm, hot	5 traffic light
5 petrol	5 rain
5 I like…	5 (to) give / given

5 più	5 strada principale
5 telefonino	5 vecchio/a
5 venire	5 contento/a
6 Salve!	6 città
6 aeroporto	6 a Natale
6 libro	6 appartamento

5 main road	5 more
5 old	5 mobile phone
5 pleased, happy	5 (to) come
6 town	6 Hello!
6 at Christmas	6 airport
6 apartment, flat	6 book

6 le riparazioni	6 laggiù
6 la neve	6 lo so
6 mai	6 vedo
6 conosciamo	6 fanno
6 invece	6 meraviglioso/a
6 spesso	6 la nave

6 down there	6 the repairs
6 I know (it)	6 the snow
6 I see	6 never, ever
6 they do	6 we know
6 wonderful	6 instead
6 the ship	6 often

Buongiorno, sono… 1

un momento per favore… 1

Andiamo a Firenze. 1

Venezia è molto bella. 1

Lavoro a Londra. 1

per la mia ditta 1

Ho bisogno di molti soldi. 1

Adesso siamo in vacanza. 1

Abbiamo una casa. 1

Sono stato/stata in Italia. 1

Good morning, I am... 1

one moment, please... 1

We go/Let's go to Florence. 1

Venice is very beautiful. 1

I work in London. 1

for my company 1

I need a lot of money. 1

We are on holiday now. 1

We have a house. 1

I was/have been in Italy. 1

Ha una camera? 2

Dov'è la camera? 2

Quanto costa? 2

a che ora 2

Vorremmo andare a Roma. 2

alle otto e mezza 2

È troppo caro. 2

C'è un bar qui? 2

qualcosa da mangiare 2

il conto per favore 2

Do you have a room? 2

Where is the room? 2

How much does it cost? 2

at what time 2

We would like to go to Rome. 2

at half past eight 2

It is too expensive. 2

Is there a bar here? 2

something to eat 2

the bill, please 2

Mi dispiace. 3

Dobbiamo andare. 3

Vorrei fare spese. 3

Devo passare dal Bankomat. 3

fino a quando 3

C'è un negozio? 3

Non importa. 3

Ho comprato troppo. 3

È molto simpatico. 3

vicino alla posta 3

I am sorry. 3

We must go. 3

I want to go shopping. 3

I must go to the Bankomat. 3

until when 3

Is there a shop? 3

It doesn't matter. 3

I have bought too much. 3

He is very nice. 3

near the post office 3

4
C'è qualcuno.

4
Non ha detto.

4
la settimana prossima

4
davanti alla porta

4
dietro alla chiesa

4
Non abbiamo tempo.

4
Andiamo a mangiare.

4
Vado con lui.

4
Mi aiuti per favore.

4
Come si dice in italiano…?

There is someone.	4
He did not say.	4
next week	4
in front of the door	4
behind the church	4
We don't have time.	4
We are going to eat.	4
I('ll) go with him.	4
Help me, please.	4
How do you say in Italian…?	4

andata e ritorno 5

Mi dispiace, non capisco. 5

Può parlare più lentamente? 5

A che ora c'è un treno? 5

Sono molto contento. 5

Mi piace la Fiat. 5

Mi piace, perché è nuovo. 5

Mi piacciono tutti e due. 5

Il vino non mi piace. 5

Si può fumare qui? 5

5 return (ticket)

5 I am sorry, I don't understand?

5 Can you speak more slowly?

5 At what time is there a train?

5 I am very happy.

5 I like the Fiat.

5 I like it because it is new.

5 I like both.

5 I don't like wine.

5 Can one smoke here?

Nessuno lo sa. 6

Non lo so. 6

Che cosa c'è? 6

Cosa ha detto? 6

Cosa fanno? 6

Come va? 6

Non vedo… 6

Non c'è niente. 6

Non sono mai stato. 6

Andiamo da un amico. 6

6
Nobody knows it.

6
I don’t know it.

6
What is it? / What is there?

6
What did he say?

6
What are they doing?

6
How are you?

6
I do not see…

6
There is nothing.

6
I have never been.

6
We are going to a friend’s.

This is to certify
that

....

has successfully completed
a six week course of

Instant Italian

with .... *results*

Elizabeth Smith

Date *Instructor*